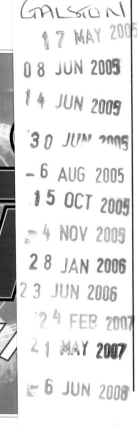

The Library
IN EAST AYRSHIRE

East Ayrshire
COUNCIL

Please return item by last date shown,
or contact library to renew

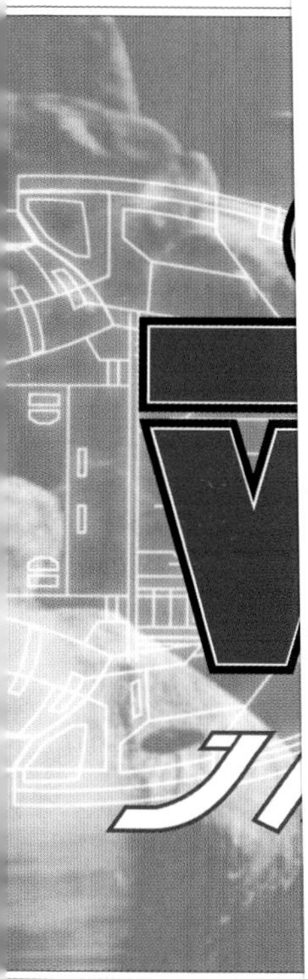

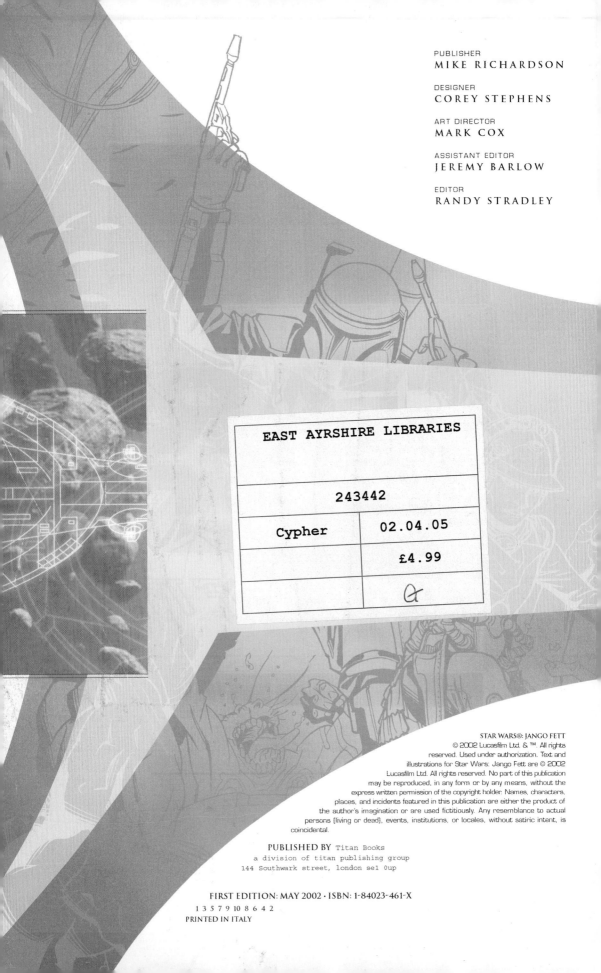

PUBLISHER
MIKE RICHARDSON

DESIGNER
COREY STEPHENS

ART DIRECTOR
MARK COX

ASSISTANT EDITOR
JEREMY BARLOW

EDITOR
RANDY STRADLEY

PUBLISHED BY Titan Books
a division of titan publishing group
144 Southwark street, london se1 0up

FIRST EDITION: MAY 2002 · ISBN: 1-84023-461-X
1 3 5 7 9 10 8 6 4 2
PRINTED IN ITALY

STAR WARS

JANGO FETT

STORY BY	RON MARZ
ART BY	TOM FOWLER
LETTERING BY	DAN JACKSON

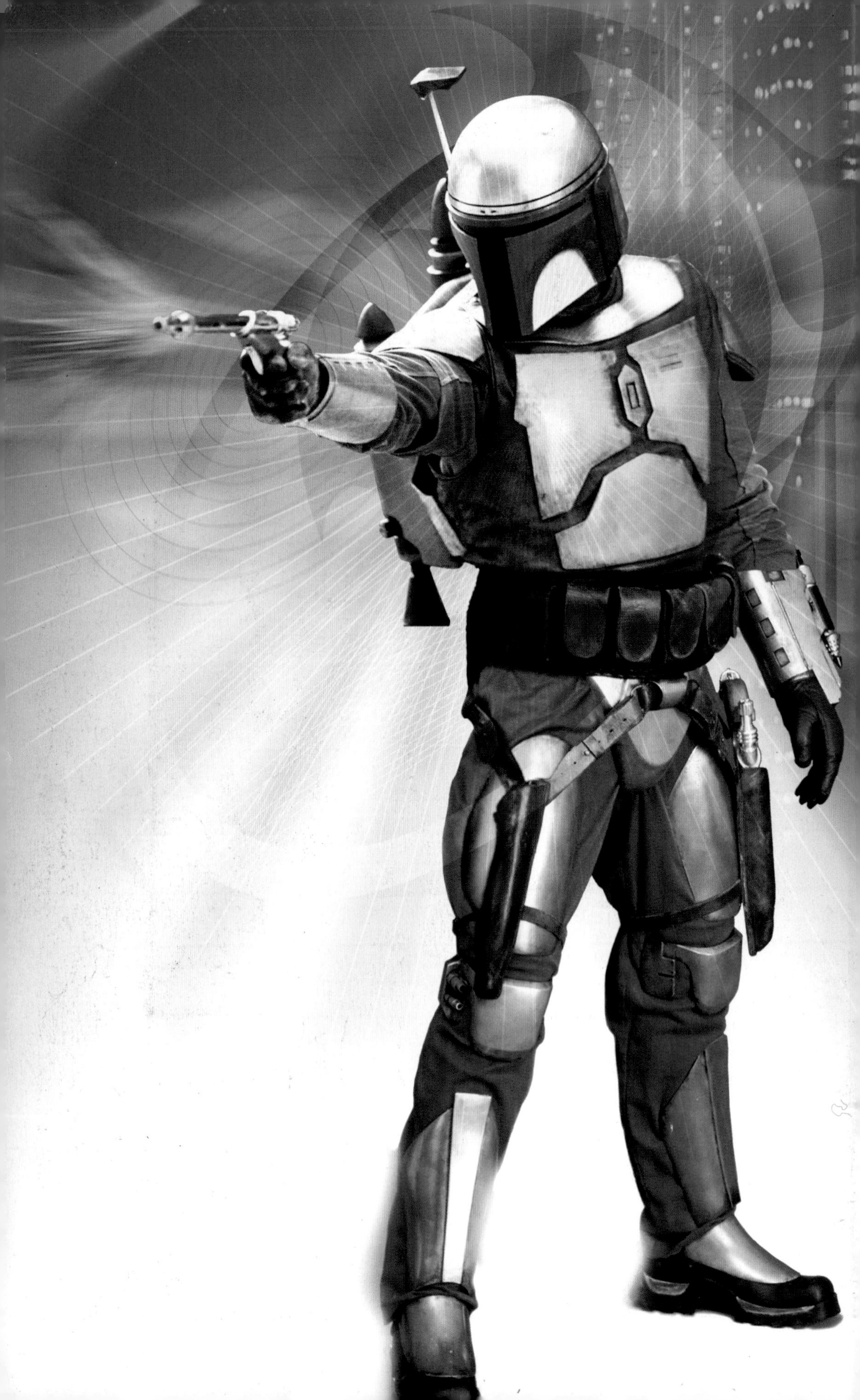

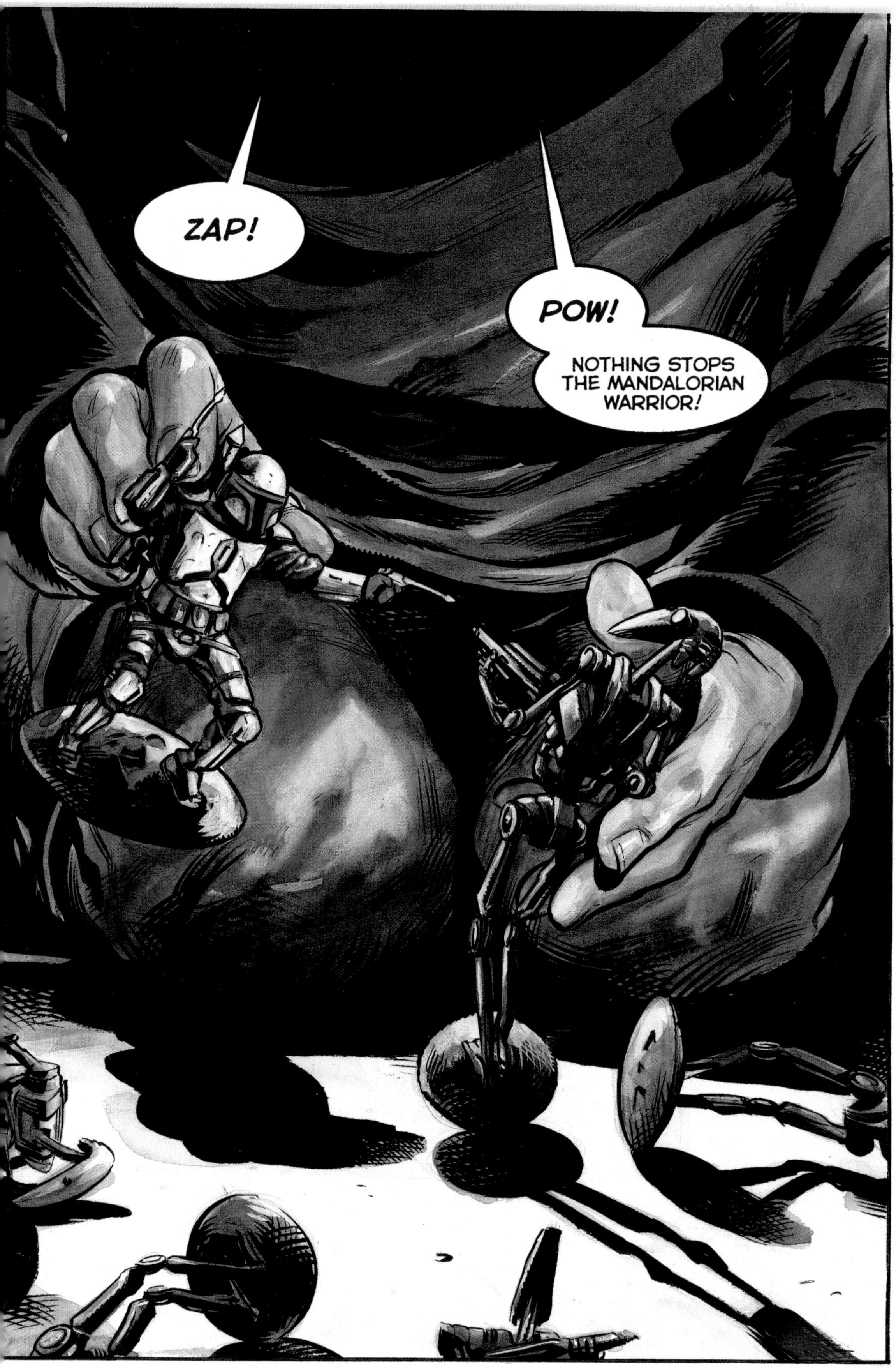
ZAP!
POW!
NOTHING STOPS THE MANDALORIAN WARRIOR!

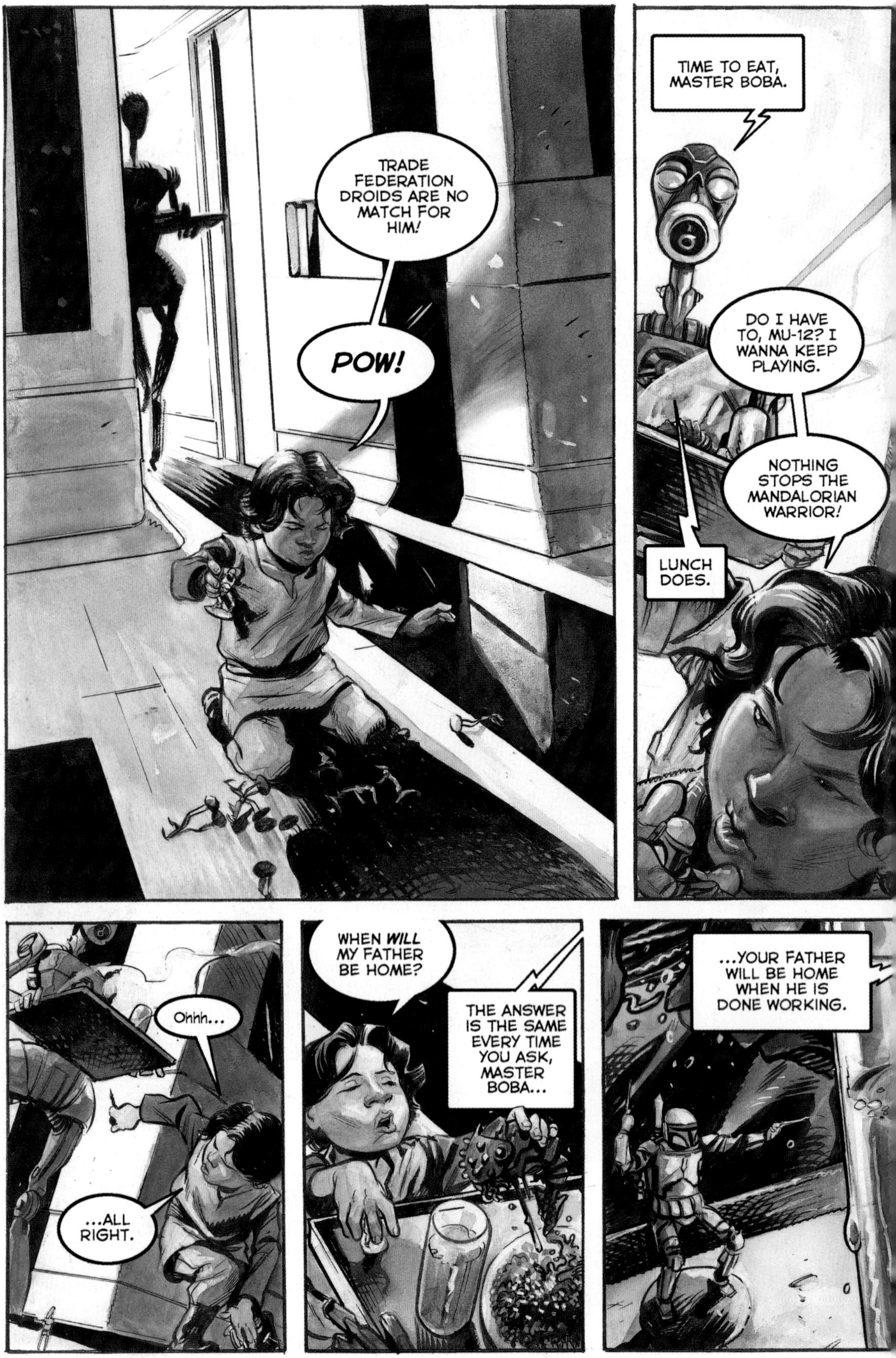
TRADE FEDERATION DROIDS ARE NO MATCH FOR HIM!
POW!
TIME TO EAT, MASTER BOBA.
DO I HAVE TO, MU-12? I WANNA KEEP PLAYING.
NOTHING STOPS THE MANDALORIAN WARRIOR!
LUNCH DOES.
Ohhh...
...ALL RIGHT.
WHEN WILL MY FATHER BE HOME?
THE ANSWER IS THE SAME EVERY TIME YOU ASK, MASTER BOBA...
...YOUR FATHER WILL BE HOME WHEN HE IS DONE WORKING.

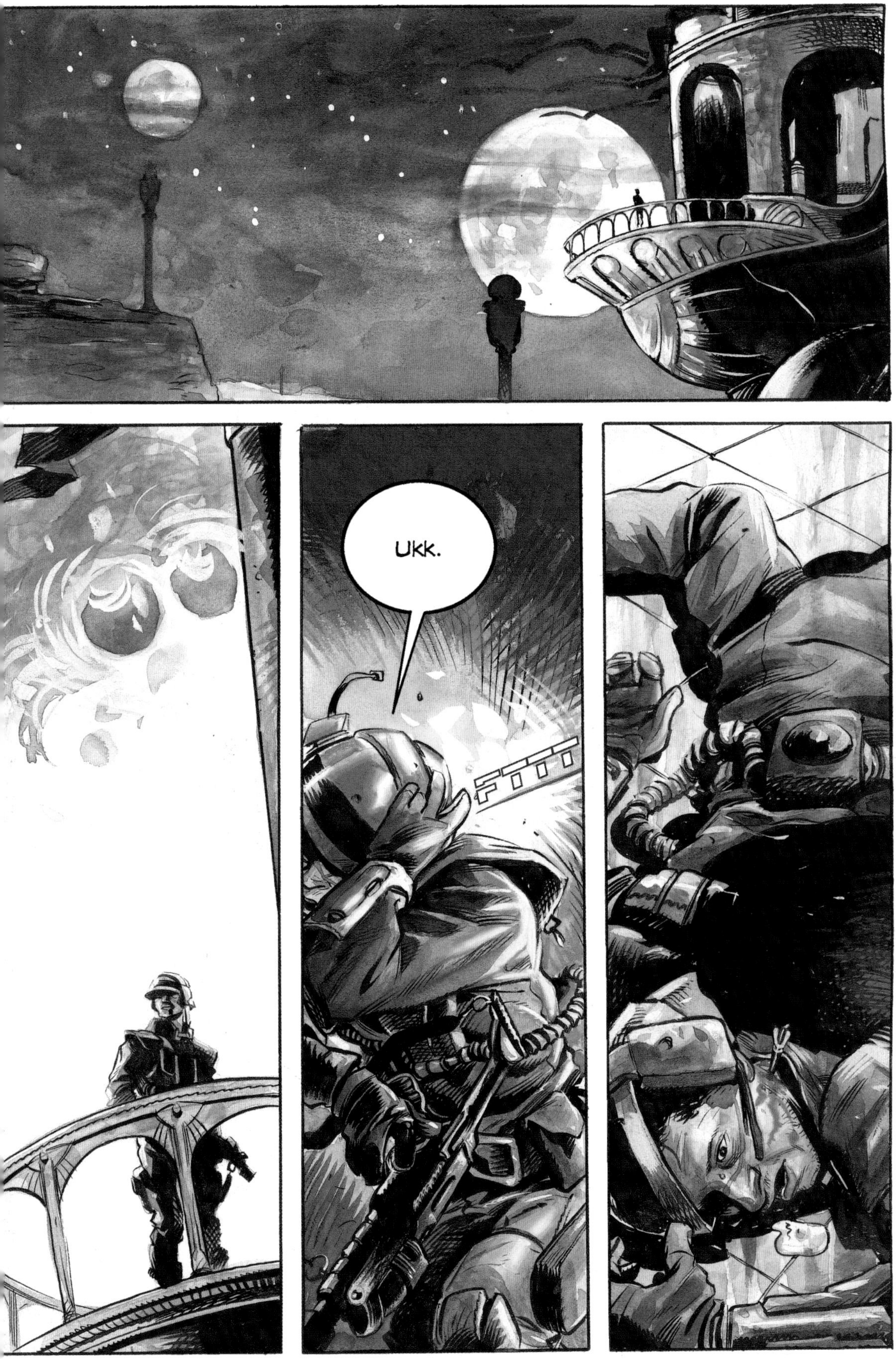
UKK.
FTTT

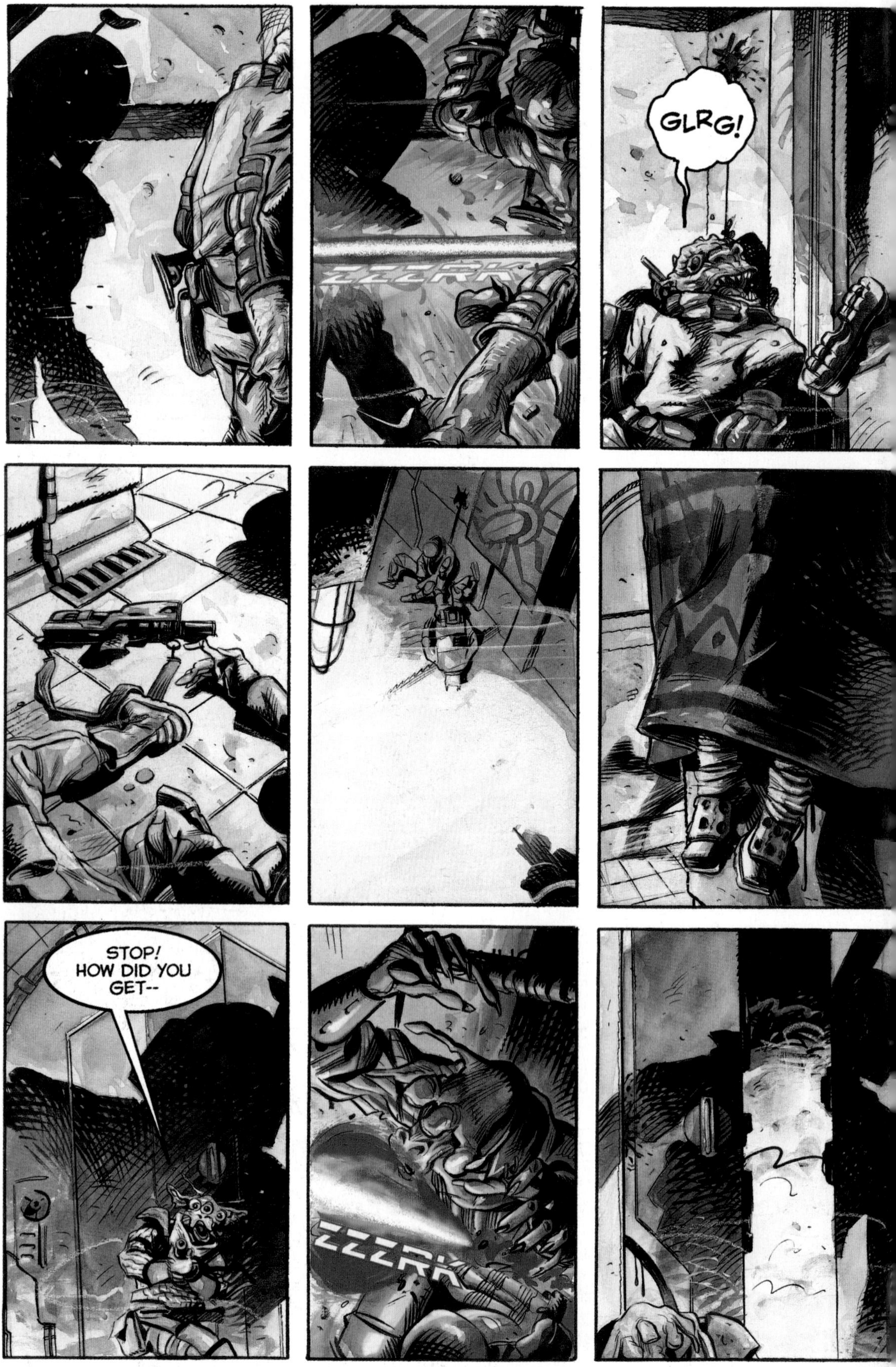
ZZZRK
GLRG!
STOP! HOW DID YOU GET--
ZZZRK

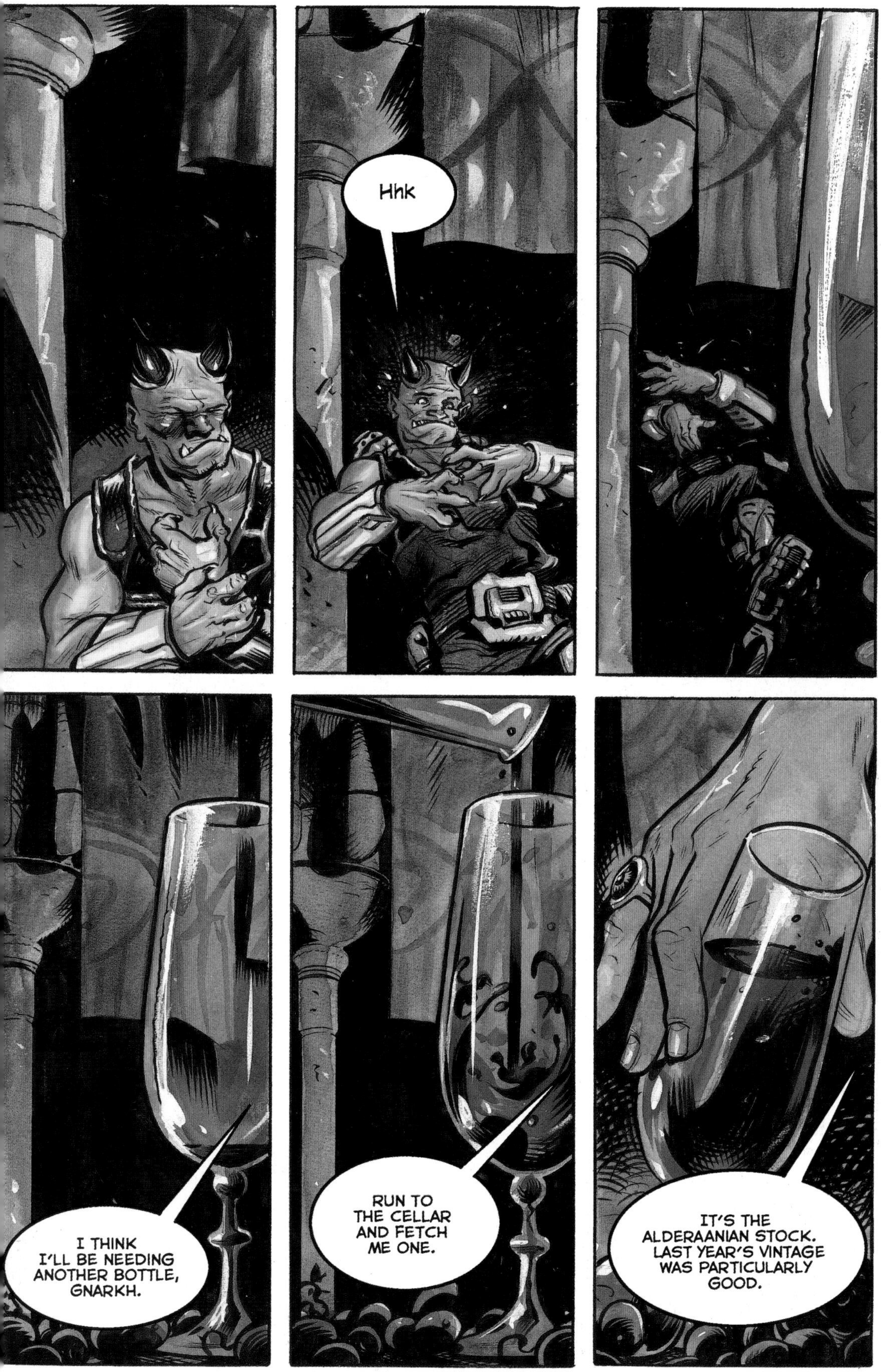
Hhk
I THINK I'LL BE NEEDING ANOTHER BOTTLE, GNARKH.
RUN TO THE CELLAR AND FETCH ME ONE.
IT'S THE ALDERAANIAN STOCK. LAST YEAR'S VINTAGE WAS PARTICULARLY GOOD.

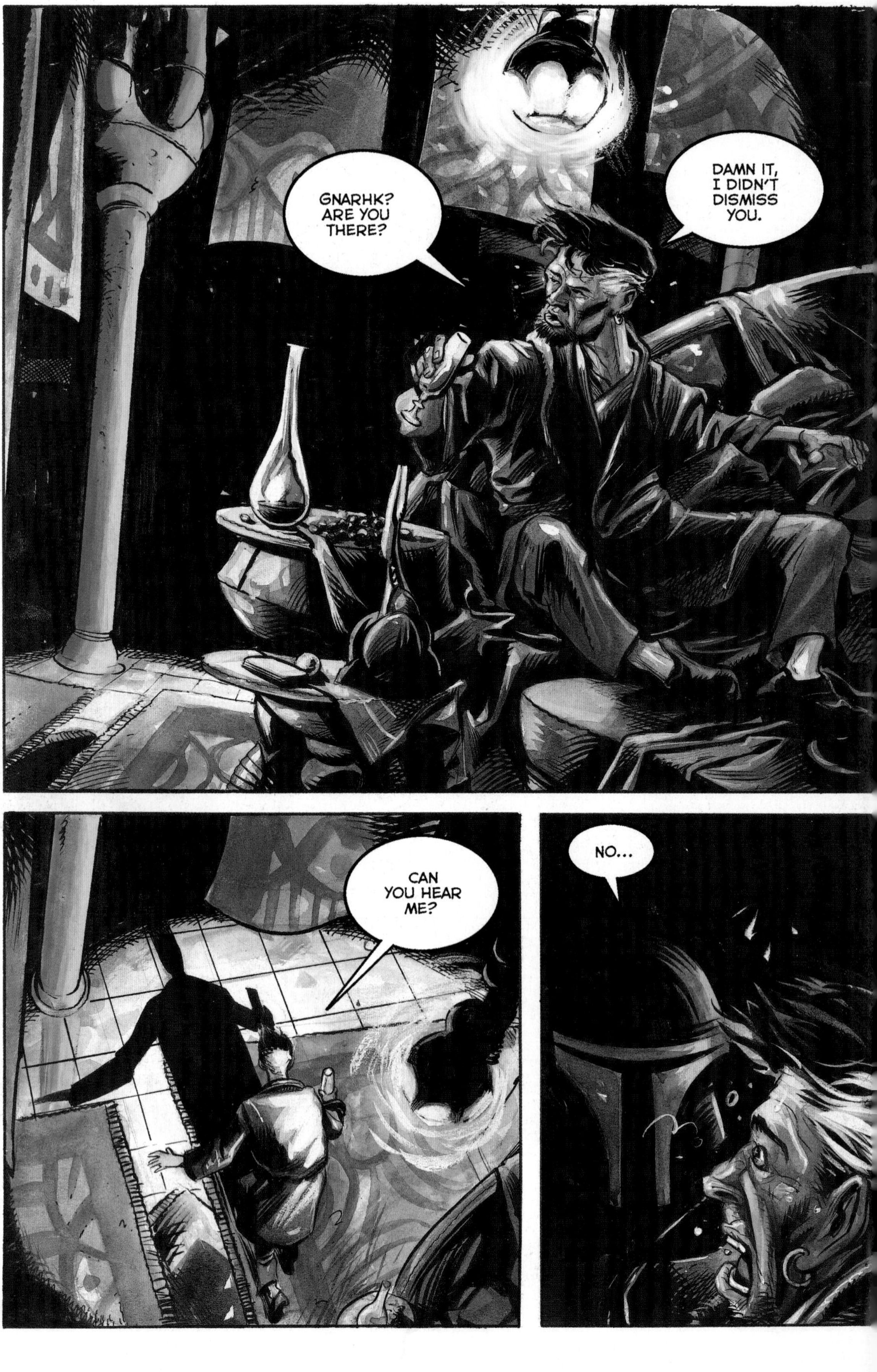
GNARHK? ARE YOU THERE?
DAMN IT, I DIDN'T DISMISS YOU.
CAN YOU HEAR ME?
NO...

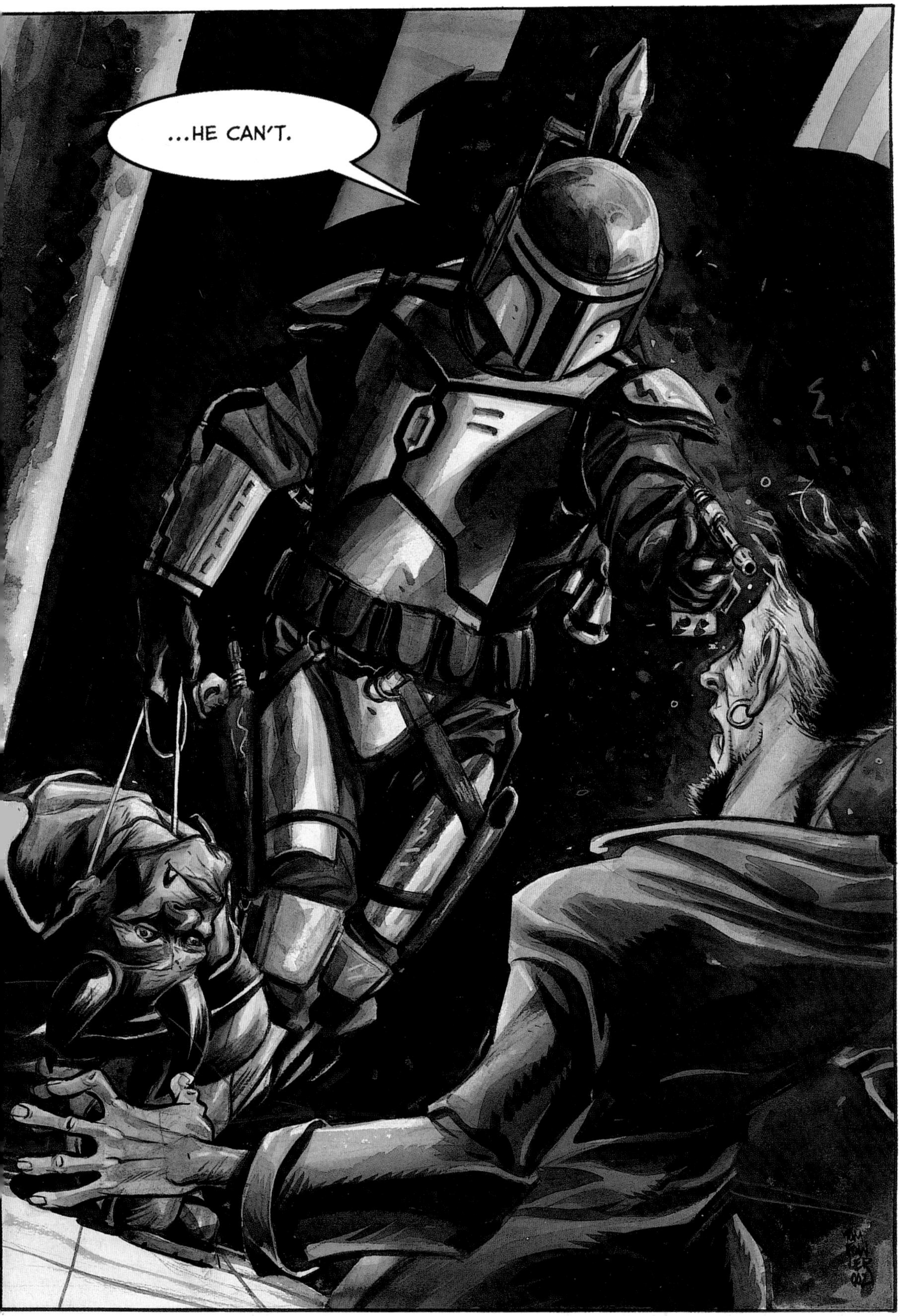
...HE CAN'T.

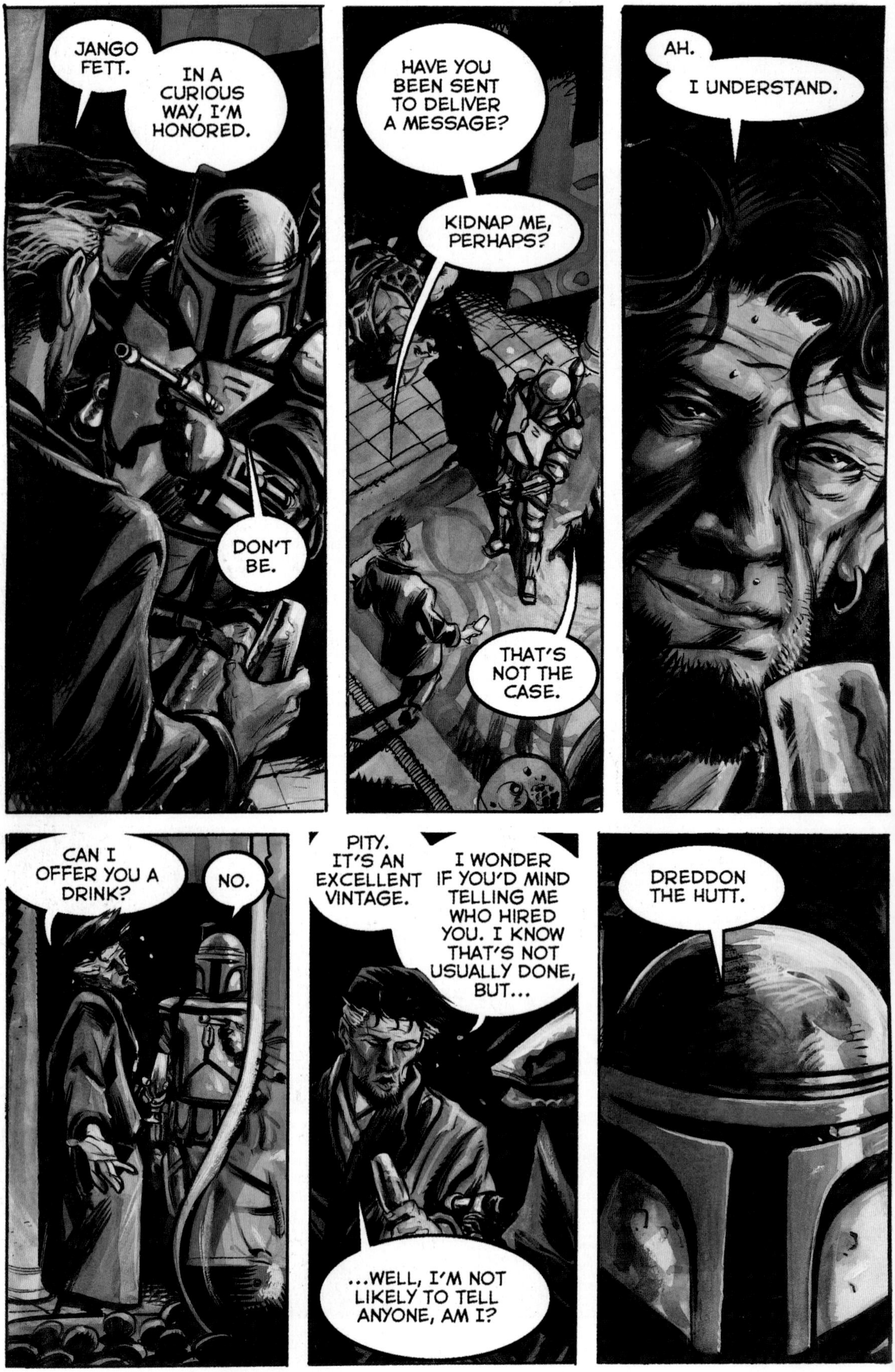
JANGO FETT.
IN A CURIOUS WAY, I'M HONORED.
DON'T BE.
HAVE YOU BEEN SENT TO DELIVER A MESSAGE?
KIDNAP ME, PERHAPS?
THAT'S NOT THE CASE.
AH.
I UNDERSTAND.
CAN I OFFER YOU A DRINK?
NO.
PITY. IT'S AN EXCELLENT VINTAGE.
I WONDER IF YOU'D MIND TELLING ME WHO HIRED YOU. I KNOW THAT'S NOT USUALLY DONE, BUT...
...WELL, I'M NOT LIKELY TO TELL ANYONE, AM I?
DREDDON THE HUTT.

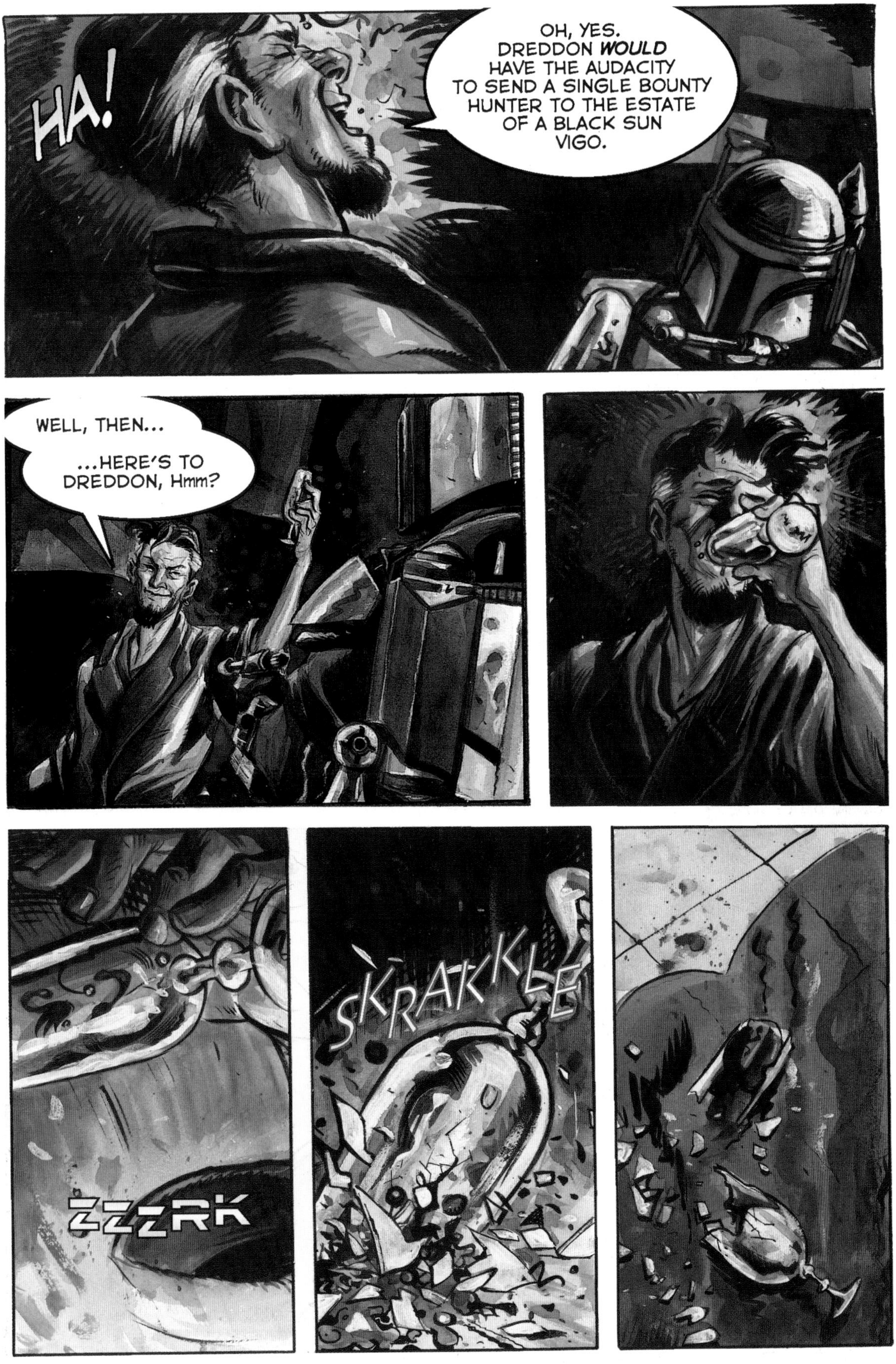
HA!
OH, YES. DREDDON WOULD HAVE THE AUDACITY TO SEND A SINGLE BOUNTY HUNTER TO THE ESTATE OF A BLACK SUN VIGO.
WELL, THEN...
...HERE'S TO DREDDON, Hmm?
ZZZRK
SKRAKKLE

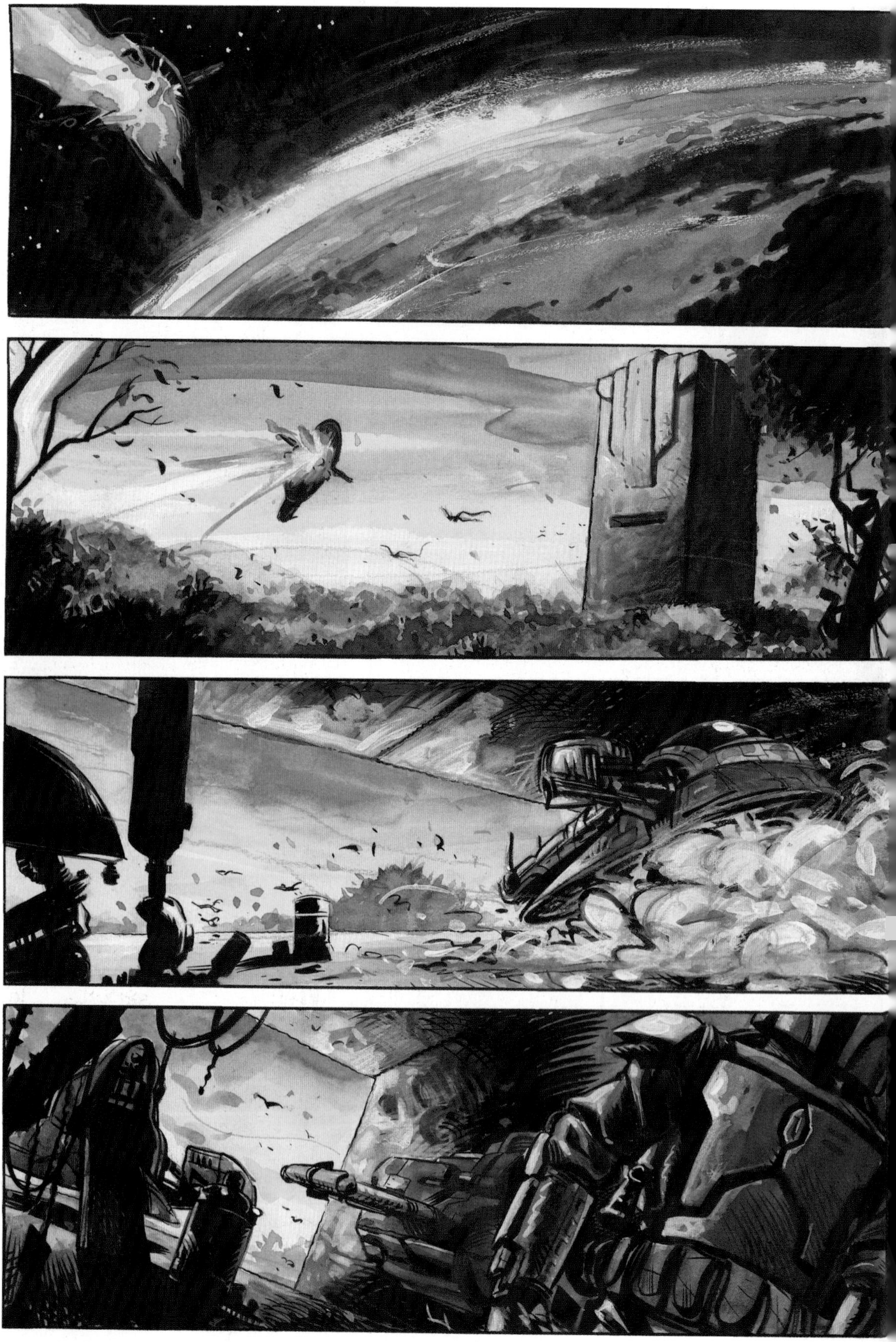

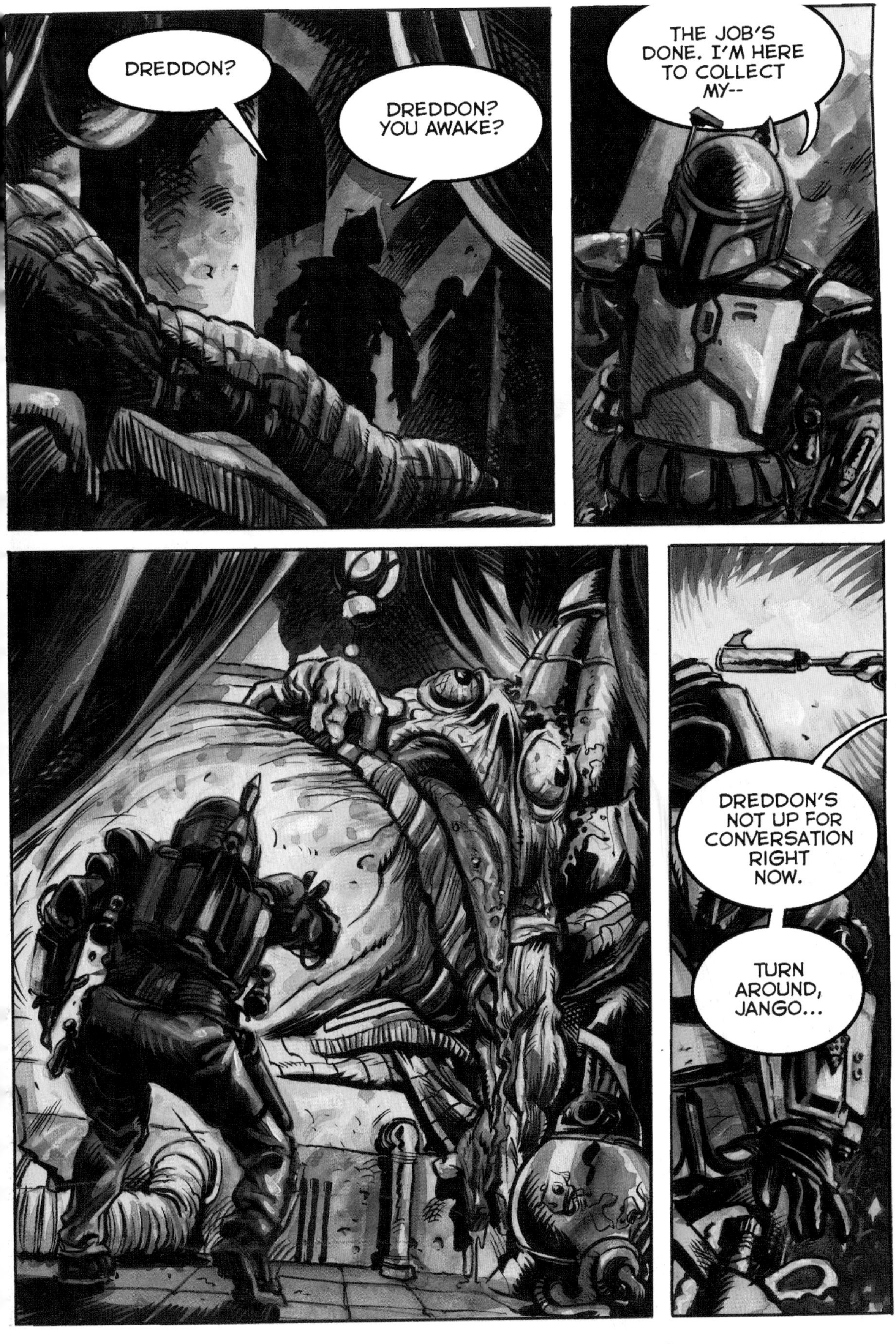
DREDDON?
DREDDON? YOU AWAKE?
THE JOB'S DONE. I'M HERE TO COLLECT MY--
DREDDON'S NOT UP FOR CONVERSATION RIGHT NOW.
TURN AROUND, JANGO...

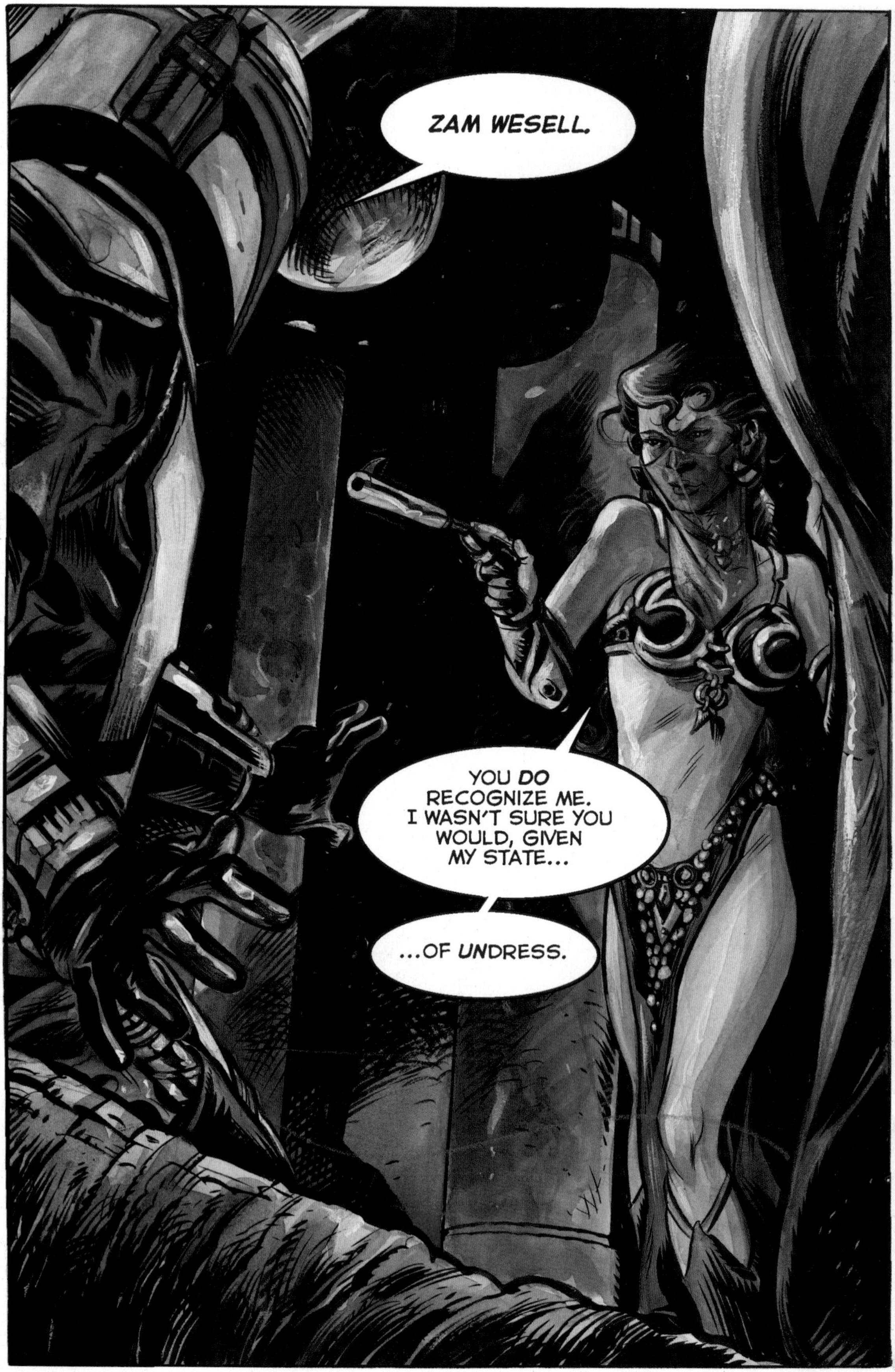
ZAM WESELL.
YOU DO RECOGNIZE ME. I WASN'T SURE YOU WOULD, GIVEN MY STATE...
...OF UNDRESS.

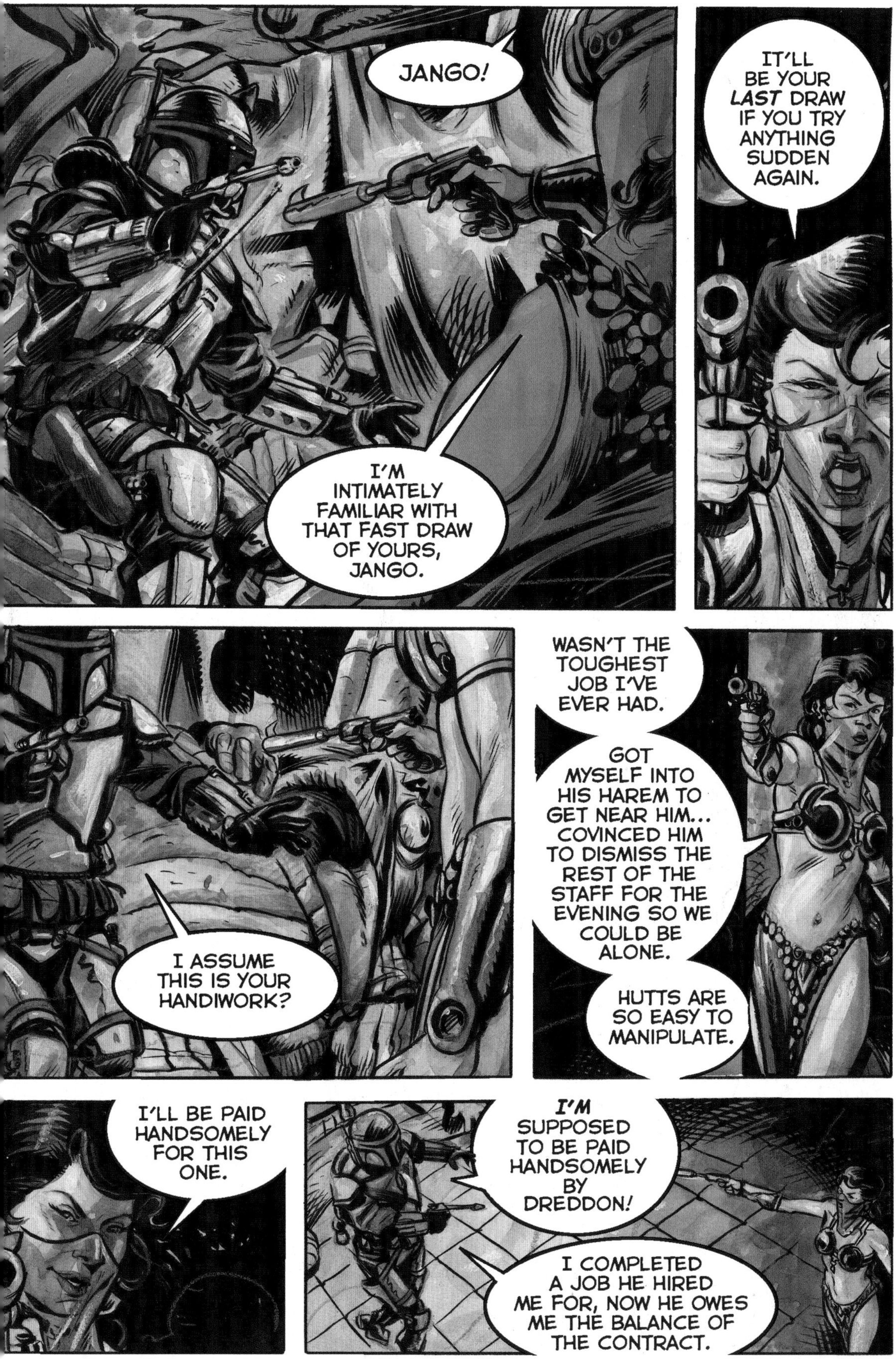
JANGO!
I'M INTIMATELY FAMILIAR WITH THAT FAST DRAW OF YOURS, JANGO.
IT'LL BE YOUR *LAST* DRAW IF YOU TRY ANYTHING SUDDEN AGAIN.
I ASSUME THIS IS YOUR HANDIWORK?
WASN'T THE TOUGHEST JOB I'VE EVER HAD.
GOT MYSELF INTO HIS HAREM TO GET NEAR HIM... COVINCED HIM TO DISMISS THE REST OF THE STAFF FOR THE EVENING SO WE COULD BE ALONE.
HUTTS ARE SO EASY TO MANIPULATE.
I'LL BE PAID HANDSOMELY FOR THIS ONE.
I'M SUPPOSED TO BE PAID HANDSOMELY BY DREDDON!
I COMPLETED A JOB HE HIRED ME FOR, NOW HE OWES ME THE BALANCE OF THE CONTRACT.

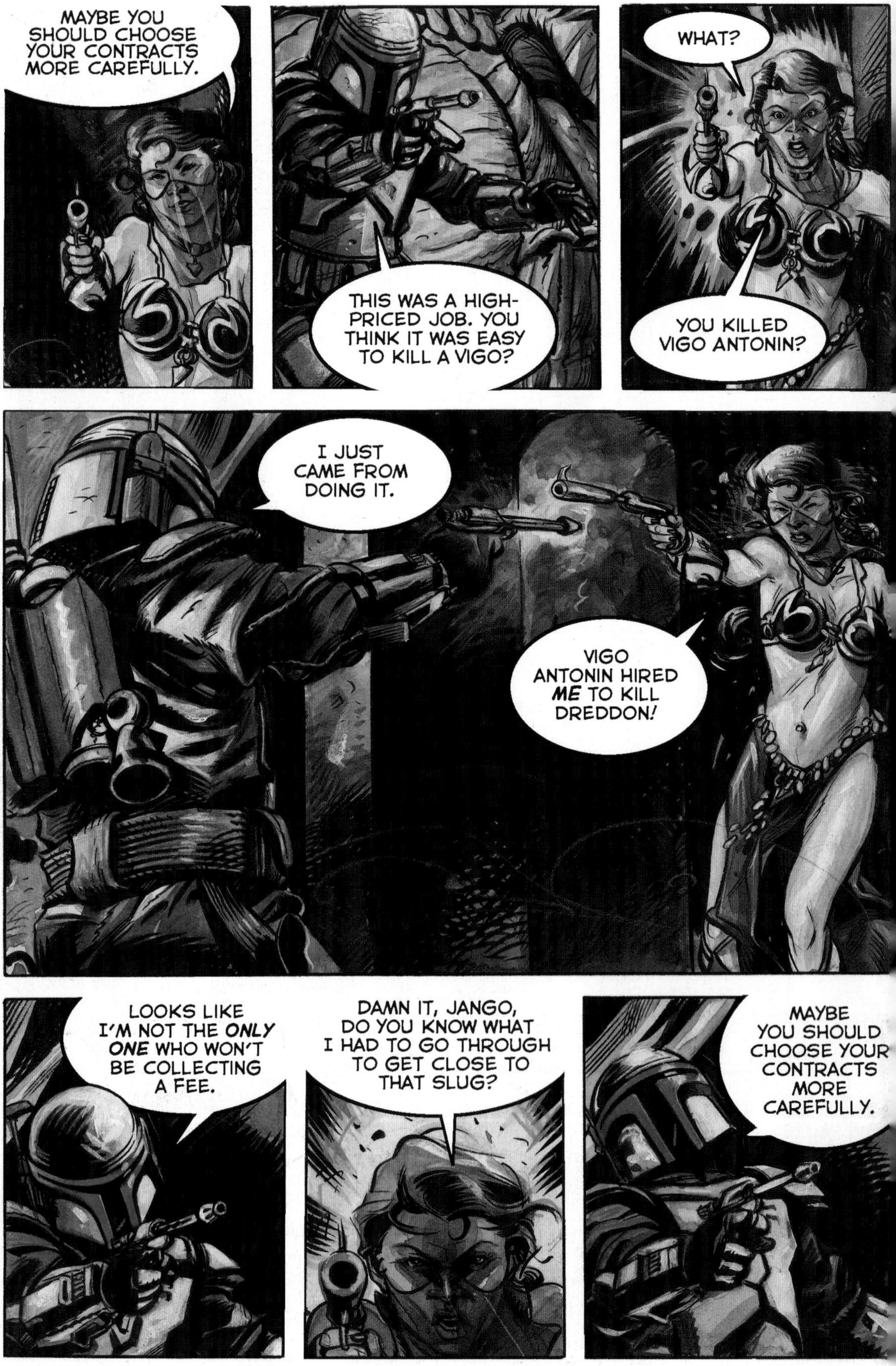
MAYBE YOU SHOULD CHOOSE YOUR CONTRACTS MORE CAREFULLY.
THIS WAS A HIGH-PRICED JOB. YOU THINK IT WAS EASY TO KILL A VIGO?
WHAT?
YOU KILLED VIGO ANTONIN?
I JUST CAME FROM DOING IT.
VIGO ANTONIN HIRED ME TO KILL DREDDON!
LOOKS LIKE I'M NOT THE ONLY ONE WHO WON'T BE COLLECTING A FEE.
DAMN IT, JANGO, DO YOU KNOW WHAT I HAD TO GO THROUGH TO GET CLOSE TO THAT SLUG?
MAYBE YOU SHOULD CHOOSE YOUR CONTRACTS MORE CAREFULLY.

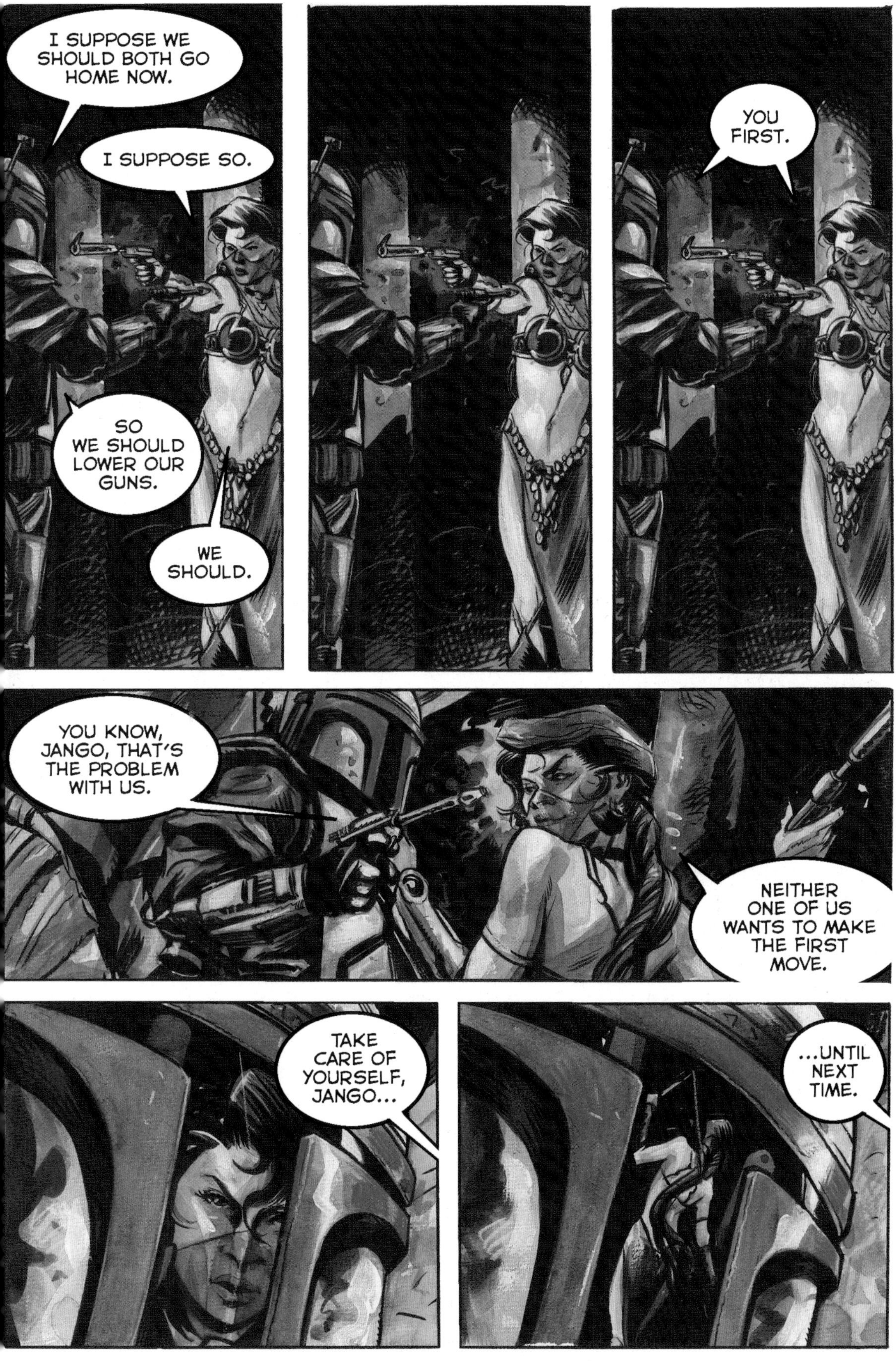
I SUPPOSE WE SHOULD BOTH GO HOME NOW.
I SUPPOSE SO.
SO WE SHOULD LOWER OUR GUNS.
WE SHOULD.
YOU FIRST.
YOU KNOW, JANGO, THAT'S THE PROBLEM WITH US.
NEITHER ONE OF US WANTS TO MAKE THE FIRST MOVE.
TAKE CARE OF YOURSELF, JANGO...
...UNTIL NEXT TIME.

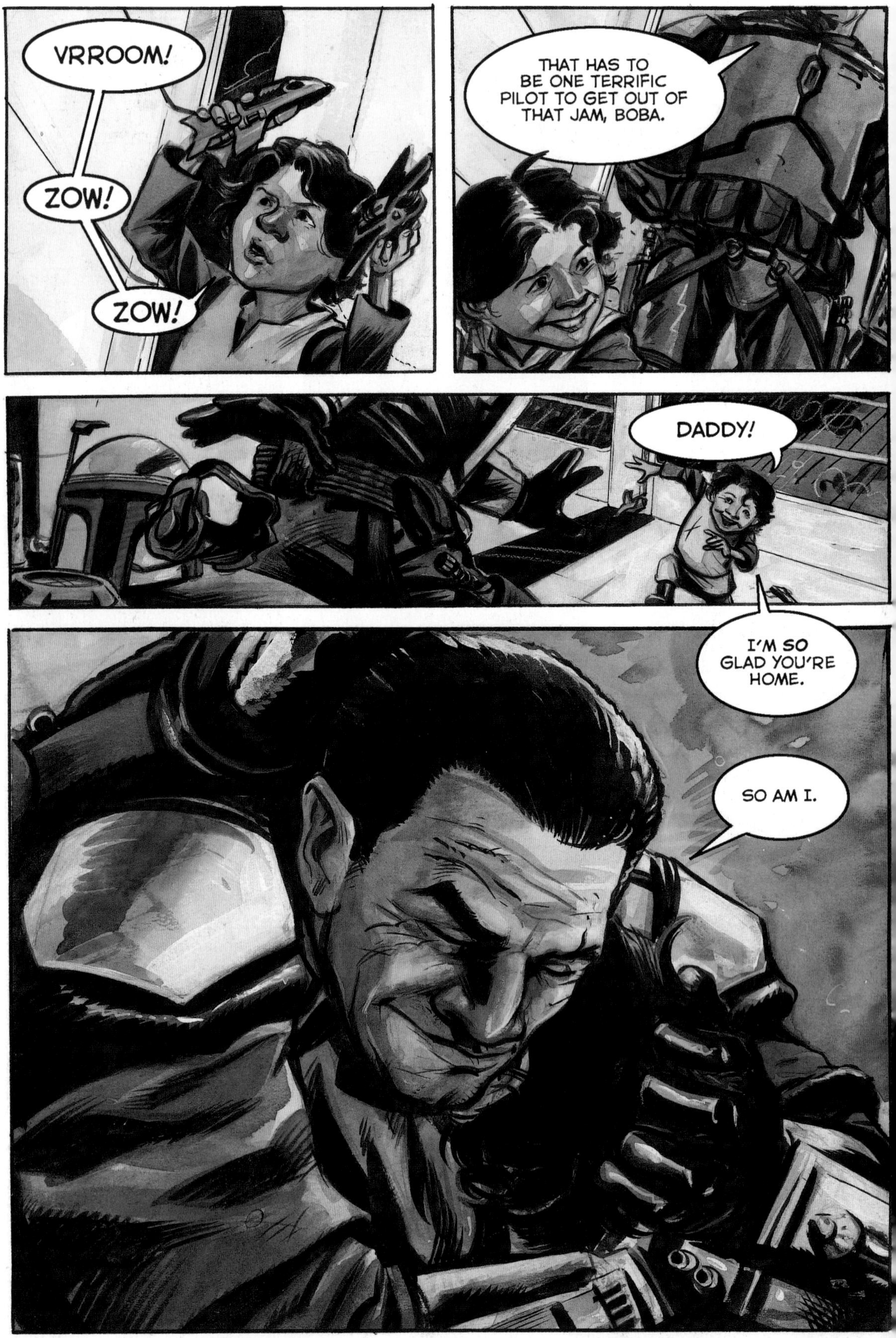
VRROOM!
ZOW!
ZOW!
THAT HAS TO BE ONE TERRIFIC PILOT TO GET OUT OF THAT JAM, BOBA.
DADDY!
I'M SO GLAD YOU'RE HOME.
SO AM I.

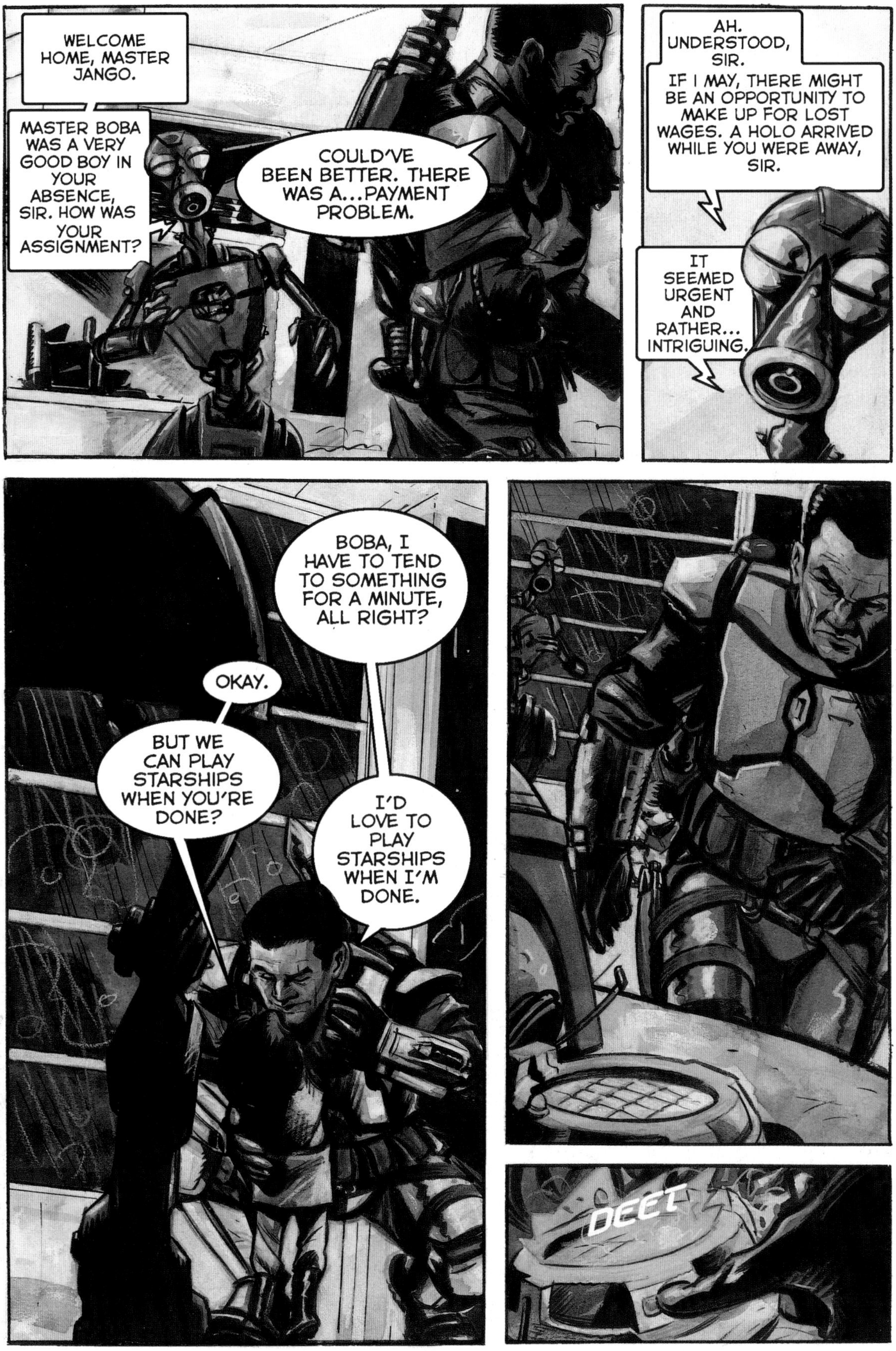
WELCOME HOME, MASTER JANGO.
MASTER BOBA WAS A VERY GOOD BOY IN YOUR ABSENCE, SIR. HOW WAS YOUR ASSIGNMENT?
COULD'VE BEEN BETTER. THERE WAS A...PAYMENT PROBLEM.
AH. UNDERSTOOD, SIR.
IF I MAY, THERE MIGHT BE AN OPPORTUNITY TO MAKE UP FOR LOST WAGES. A HOLO ARRIVED WHILE YOU WERE AWAY, SIR.
IT SEEMED URGENT AND RATHER... INTRIGUING.
BOBA, I HAVE TO TEND TO SOMETHING FOR A MINUTE, ALL RIGHT?
OKAY.
BUT WE CAN PLAY STARSHIPS WHEN YOU'RE DONE?
I'D LOVE TO PLAY STARSHIPS WHEN I'M DONE.
DEET

GREETINGS JANGO FETT.

I AM FERNOODA.

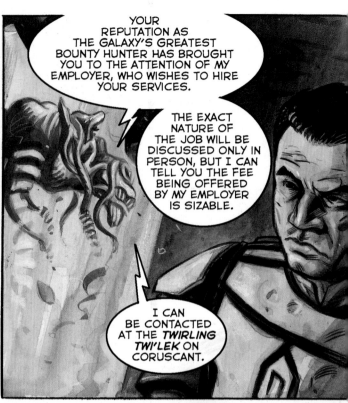

YOUR REPUTATION AS THE GALAXY'S GREATEST BOUNTY HUNTER HAS BROUGHT YOU TO THE ATTENTION OF MY EMPLOYER, WHO WISHES TO HIRE YOUR SERVICES.

THE EXACT NATURE OF THE JOB WILL BE DISCUSSED ONLY IN PERSON, BUT I CAN TELL YOU THE FEE BEING OFFERED BY MY EMPLOYER IS SIZABLE.

I CAN BE CONTACTED AT THE *TWIRLING TWI'LEK* ON CORUSCANT.

I'LL AWAIT YOU THERE.

WILL YOU BE TAKING THE JOB, SIR?

I'D RATHER NOT...

...I'D RATHER STAY HERE ON *KAMINO* WITH BOBA.

IT'S NOT RIGHT TO LEAVE AGAIN SO SOON...

...BUT I DO HAVE TO MAKE UP FOR LOST PROFITS ON THE LAST JOB.

BOBA... ...WE NEED TO TALK.

YOU'RE GOING AWAY AGAIN, AREN'T YOU?

YOU JUST GOT HOME BUT YOU'RE GOING AWAY AGAIN.

I... ...YES.

SOMETHING'S COME UP AND I NEED TO TEND TO IT. I'M SORRY, SON. I SHOULDN'T BE GONE LONG.

IT DOESN'T MEAN I LOVE YOU ANY LESS. YOU UNDERSTAND THAT, DON'T YOU?

I UNDERSTAND, BUT... ...DO YOU HAVE TO GO RIGHT NOW?

NO...

"...NOT RIGHT NOW"

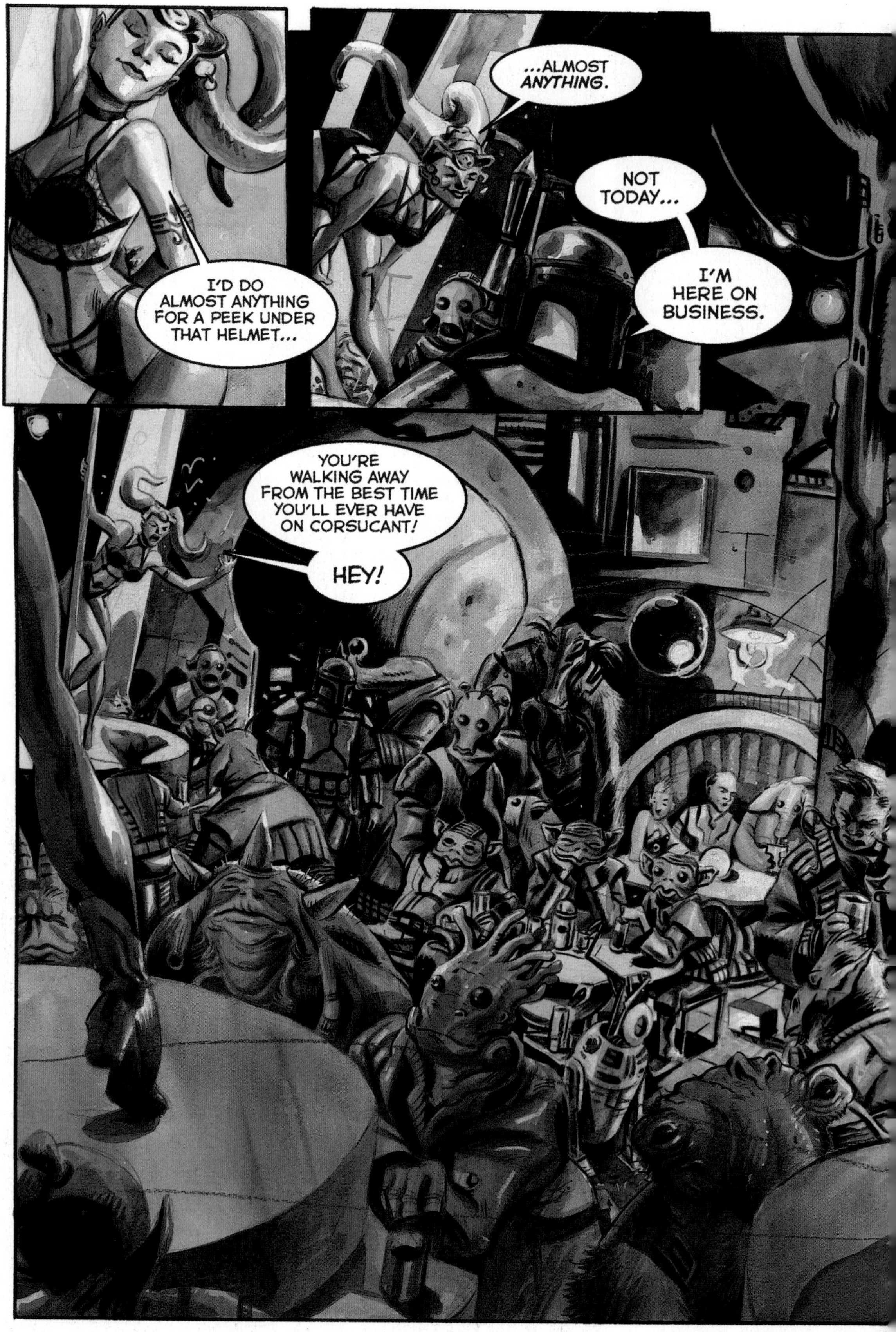
I'D DO ALMOST ANYTHING FOR A PEEK UNDER THAT HELMET...
...ALMOST ANYTHING.
NOT TODAY...
I'M HERE ON BUSINESS.
YOU'RE WALKING AWAY FROM THE BEST TIME YOU'LL EVER HAVE ON CORSUCANT!
HEY!

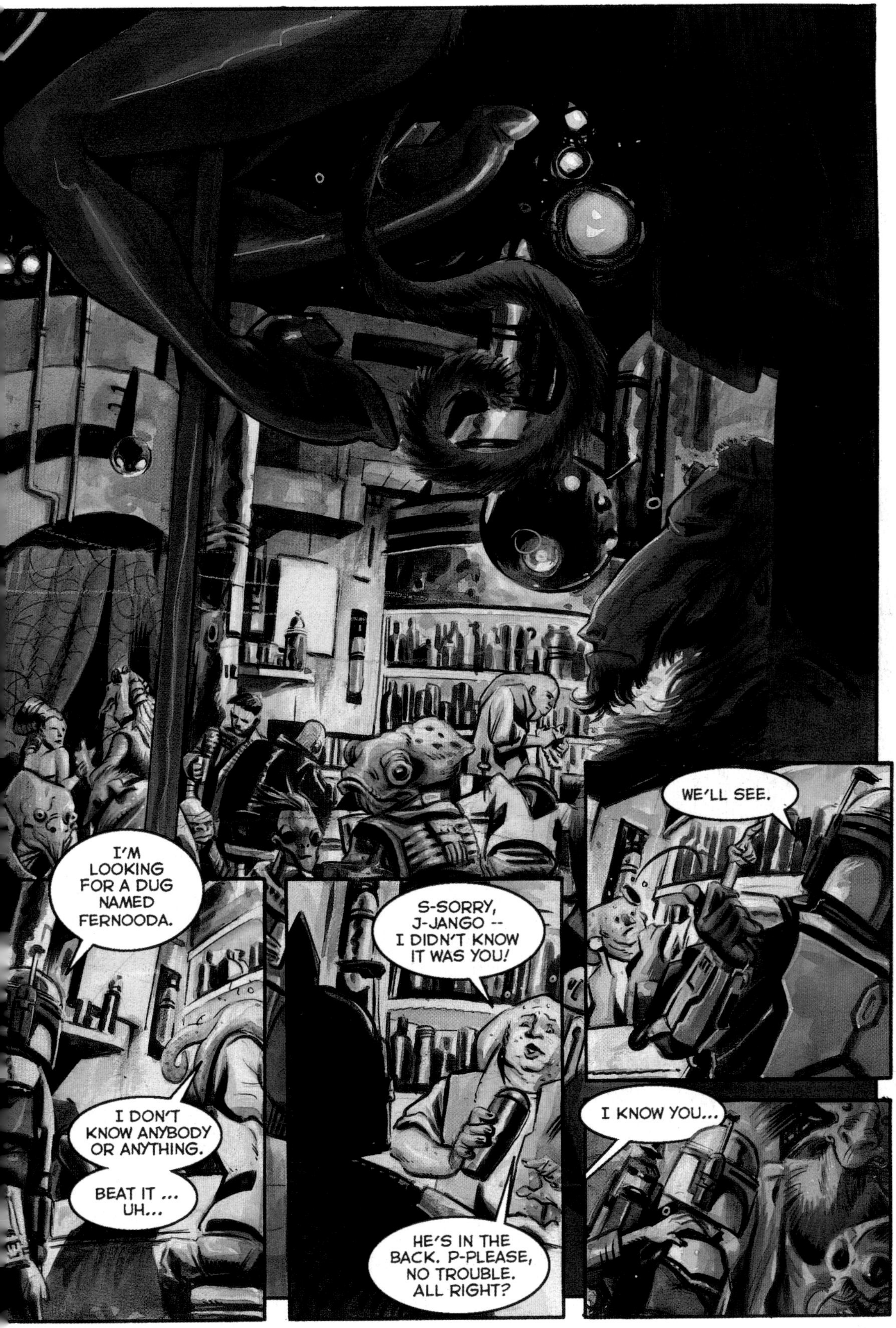
I'M LOOKING FOR A DUG NAMED FERNOODA.
I DON'T KNOW ANYBODY OR ANYTHING.
BEAT IT ... UH...
S-SORRY, J-JANGO -- I DIDN'T KNOW IT WAS YOU!
HE'S IN THE BACK. P-PLEASE, NO TROUBLE. ALL RIGHT?
WE'LL SEE.
I KNOW YOU...

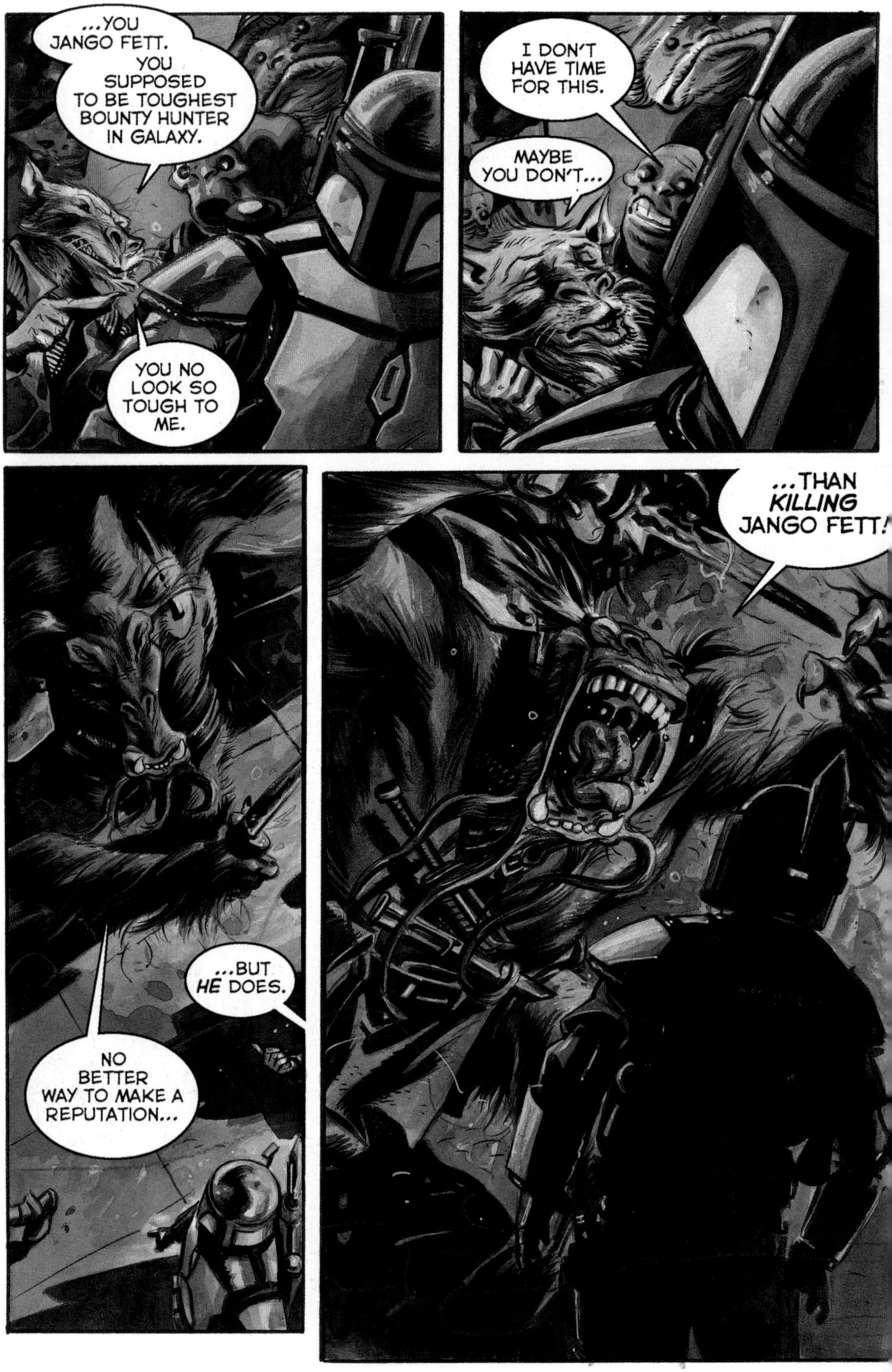
...YOU JANGO FETT.
YOU SUPPOSED TO BE TOUGHEST BOUNTY HUNTER IN GALAXY.
YOU NO LOOK SO TOUGH TO ME.
I DON'T HAVE TIME FOR THIS.
MAYBE YOU DON'T...
...BUT HE DOES.
NO BETTER WAY TO MAKE A REPUTATION...
...THAN KILLING JANGO FETT!

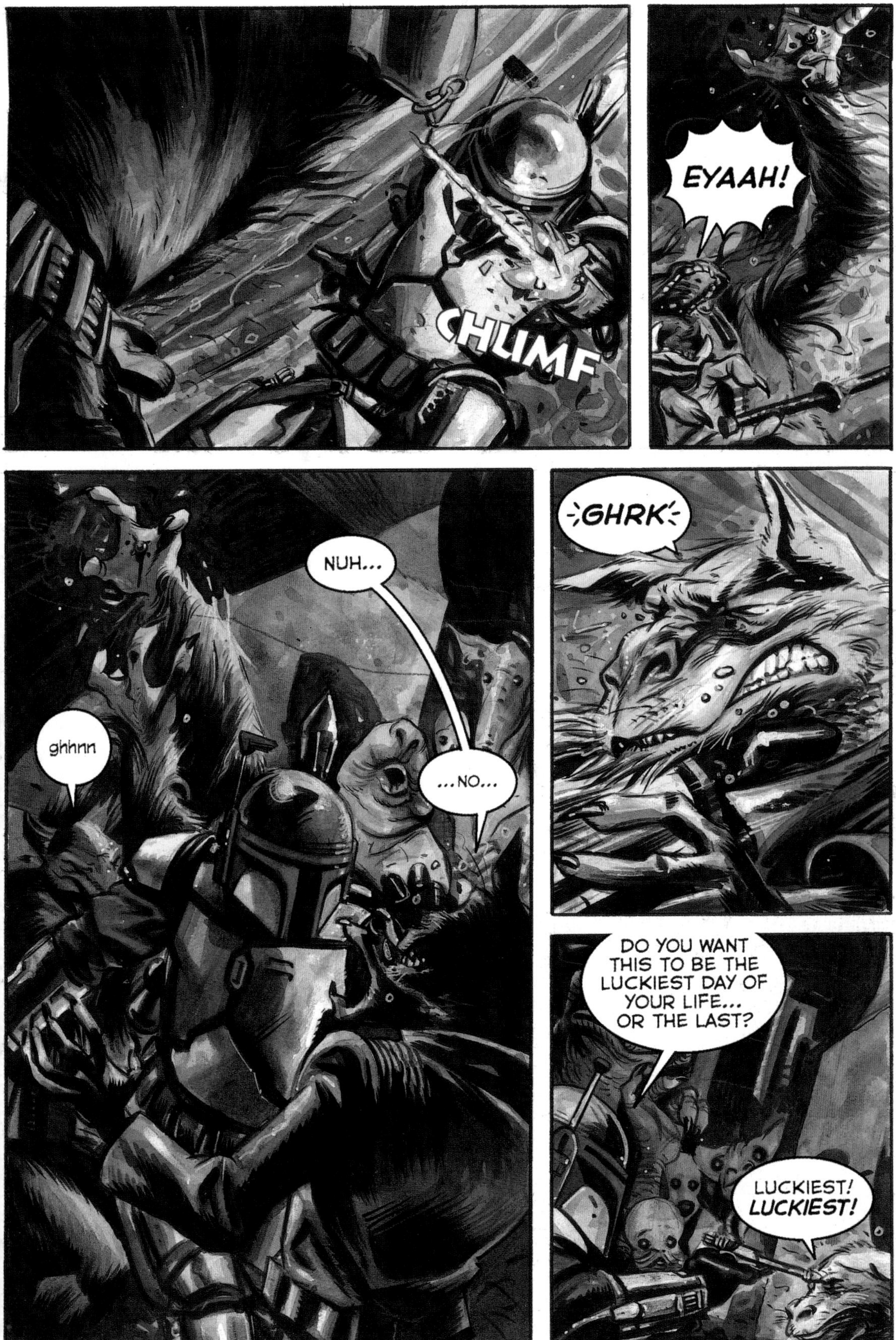
CHUMF
EYAAH!
NUH...
ghhnn
...NO...
GHRK
DO YOU WANT THIS TO BE THE LUCKIEST DAY OF YOUR LIFE... OR THE LAST?
LUCKIEST! LUCKIEST!

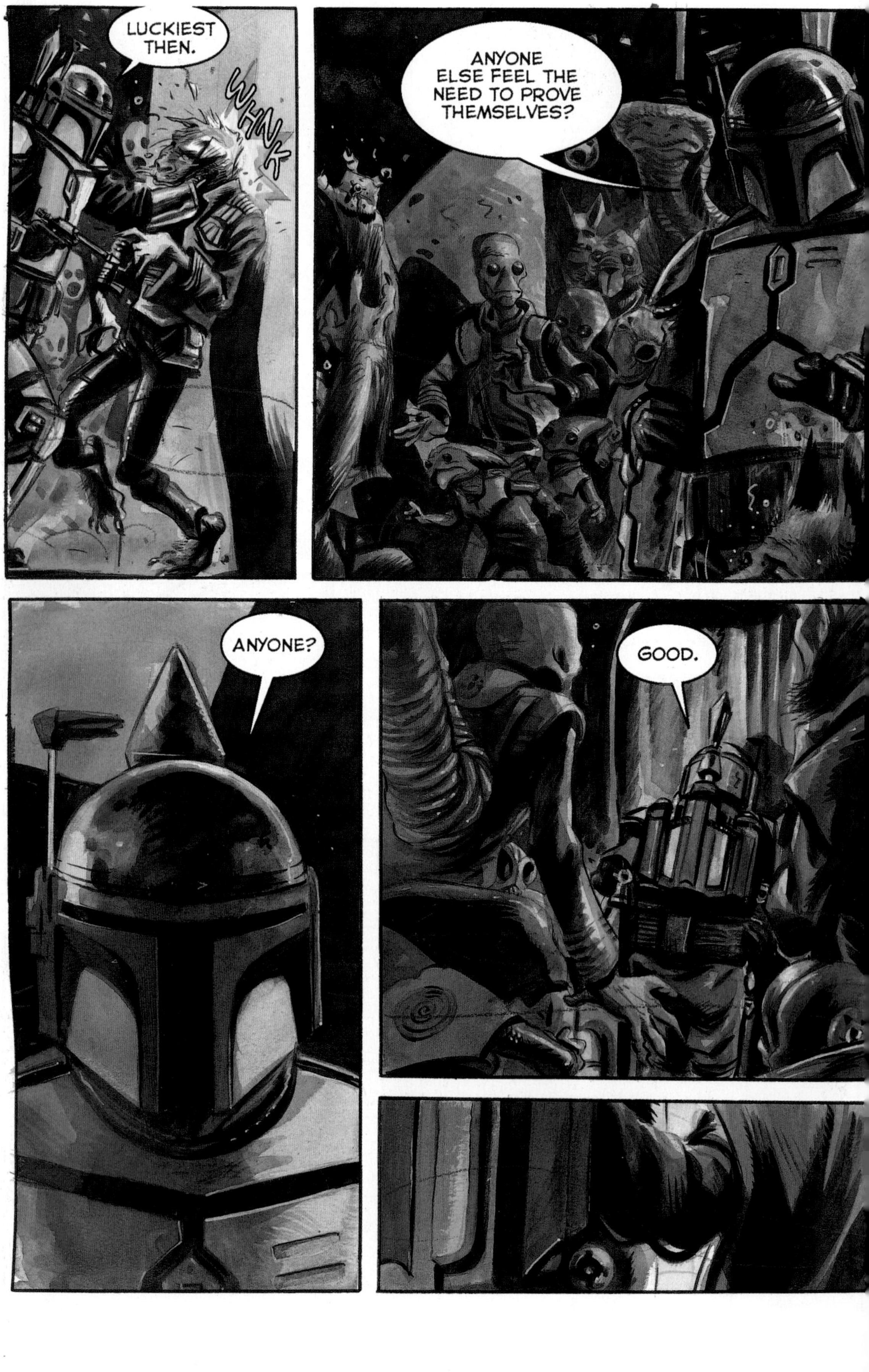
LUCKIEST THEN.
WHNK
ANYONE ELSE FEEL THE NEED TO PROVE THEMSELVES?
ANYONE?
GOOD.

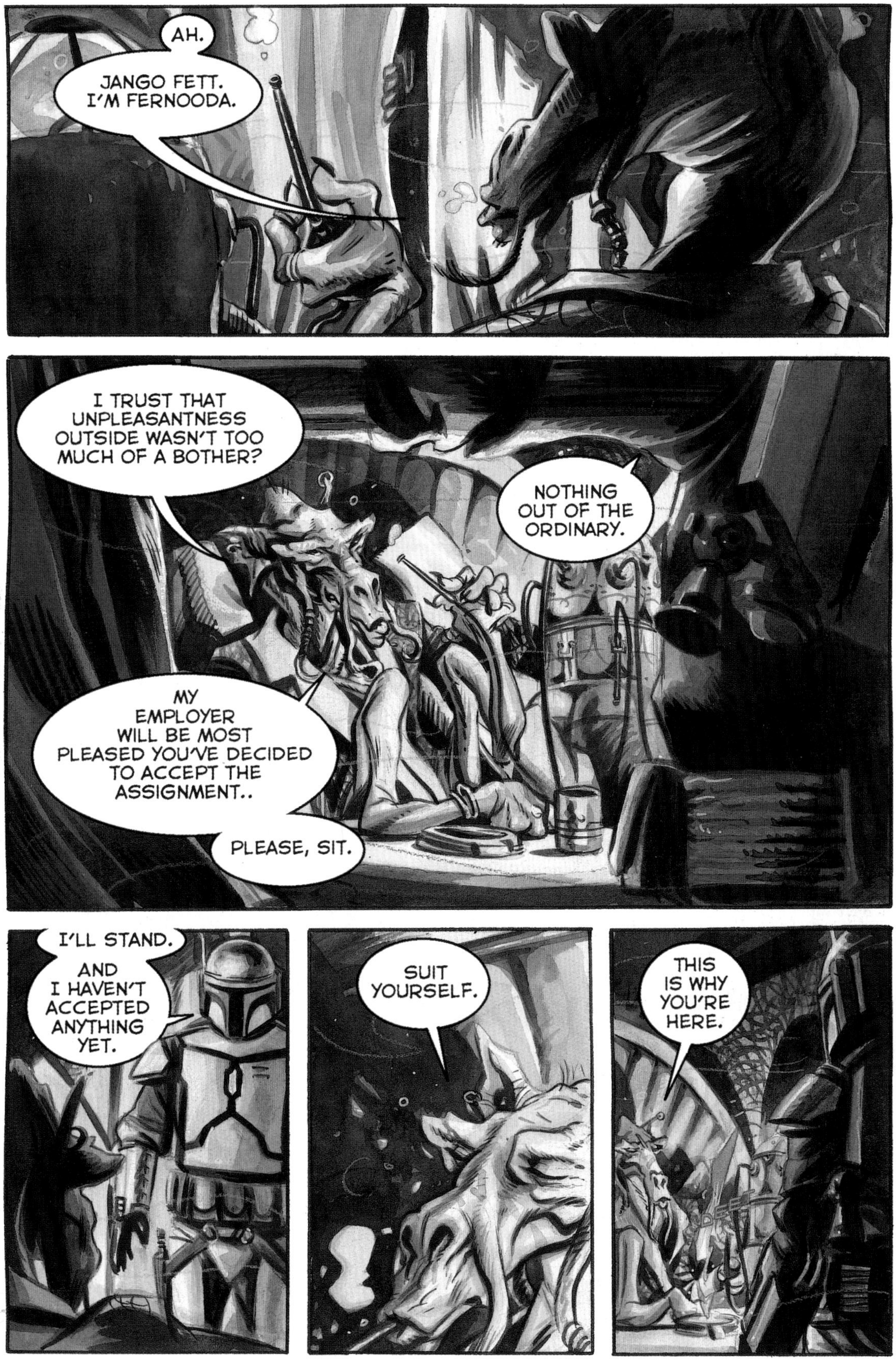
AH.
JANGO FETT. I'M FERNOODA.
I TRUST THAT UNPLEASANTNESS OUTSIDE WASN'T TOO MUCH OF A BOTHER?
NOTHING OUT OF THE ORDINARY.
MY EMPLOYER WILL BE MOST PLEASED YOU'VE DECIDED TO ACCEPT THE ASSIGNMENT..
PLEASE, SIT.
I'LL STAND.
AND I HAVEN'T ACCEPTED ANYTHING YET.
SUIT YOURSELF.
THIS IS WHY YOU'RE HERE.

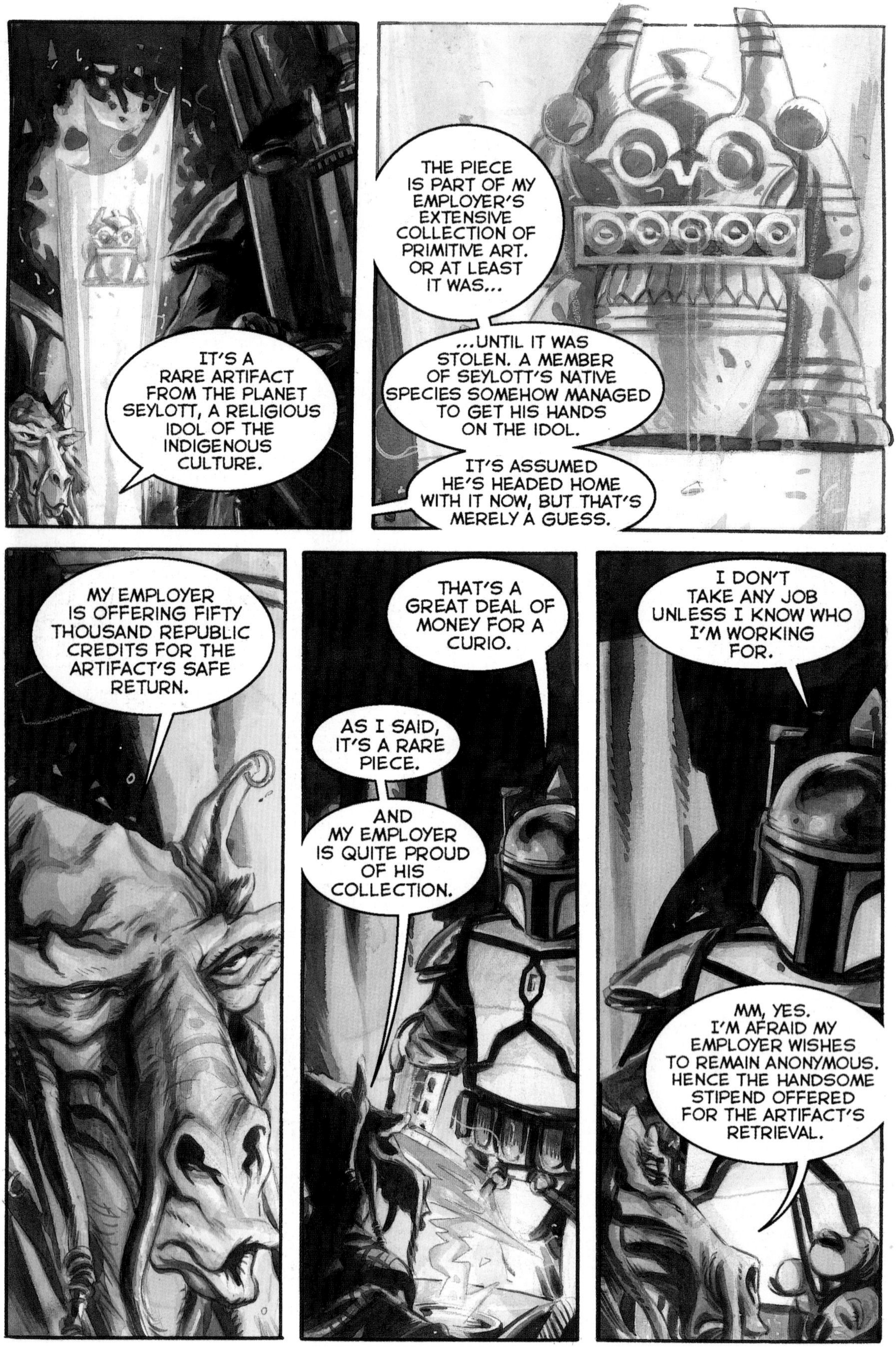
IT'S A RARE ARTIFACT FROM THE PLANET SEYLOTT, A RELIGIOUS IDOL OF THE INDIGENOUS CULTURE.
THE PIECE IS PART OF MY EMPLOYER'S EXTENSIVE COLLECTION OF PRIMITIVE ART. OR AT LEAST IT WAS...
...UNTIL IT WAS STOLEN. A MEMBER OF SEYLOTT'S NATIVE SPECIES SOMEHOW MANAGED TO GET HIS HANDS ON THE IDOL.
IT'S ASSUMED HE'S HEADED HOME WITH IT NOW, BUT THAT'S MERELY A GUESS.
MY EMPLOYER IS OFFERING FIFTY THOUSAND REPUBLIC CREDITS FOR THE ARTIFACT'S SAFE RETURN.
THAT'S A GREAT DEAL OF MONEY FOR A CURIO.
AS I SAID, IT'S A RARE PIECE.
AND MY EMPLOYER IS QUITE PROUD OF HIS COLLECTION.
I DON'T TAKE ANY JOB UNLESS I KNOW WHO I'M WORKING FOR.
MM, YES. I'M AFRAID MY EMPLOYER WISHES TO REMAIN ANONYMOUS. HENCE THE HANDSOME STIPEND OFFERED FOR THE ARTIFACT'S RETRIEVAL.

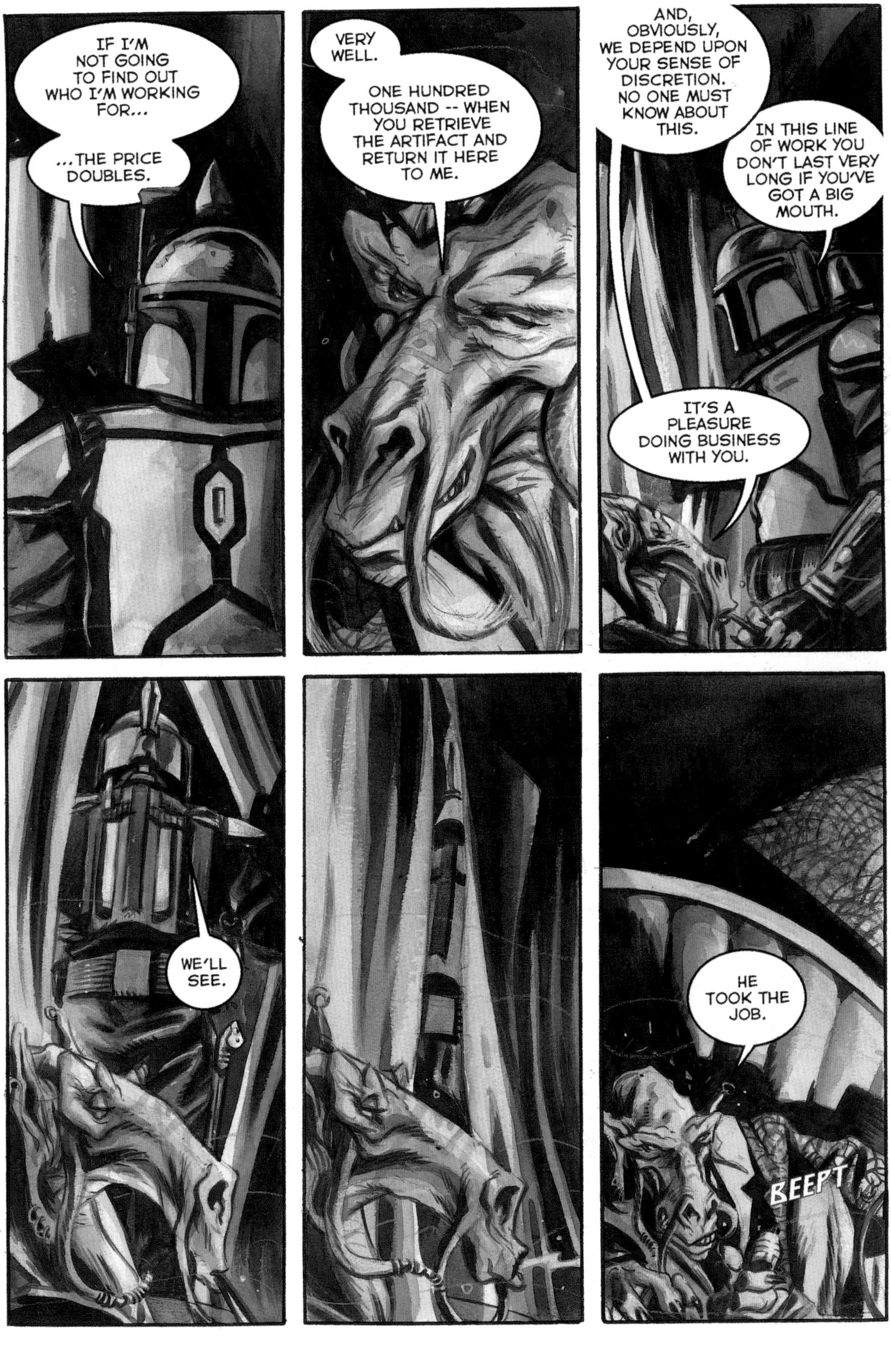
IF I'M NOT GOING TO FIND OUT WHO I'M WORKING FOR...
...THE PRICE DOUBLES.
VERY WELL.
ONE HUNDRED THOUSAND -- WHEN YOU RETRIEVE THE ARTIFACT AND RETURN IT HERE TO ME.
AND, OBVIOUSLY, WE DEPEND UPON YOUR SENSE OF DISCRETION. NO ONE MUST KNOW ABOUT THIS.
IN THIS LINE OF WORK YOU DON'T LAST VERY LONG IF YOU'VE GOT A BIG MOUTH.
IT'S A PLEASURE DOING BUSINESS WITH YOU.
WE'LL SEE.
HE TOOK THE JOB.
BEEPT

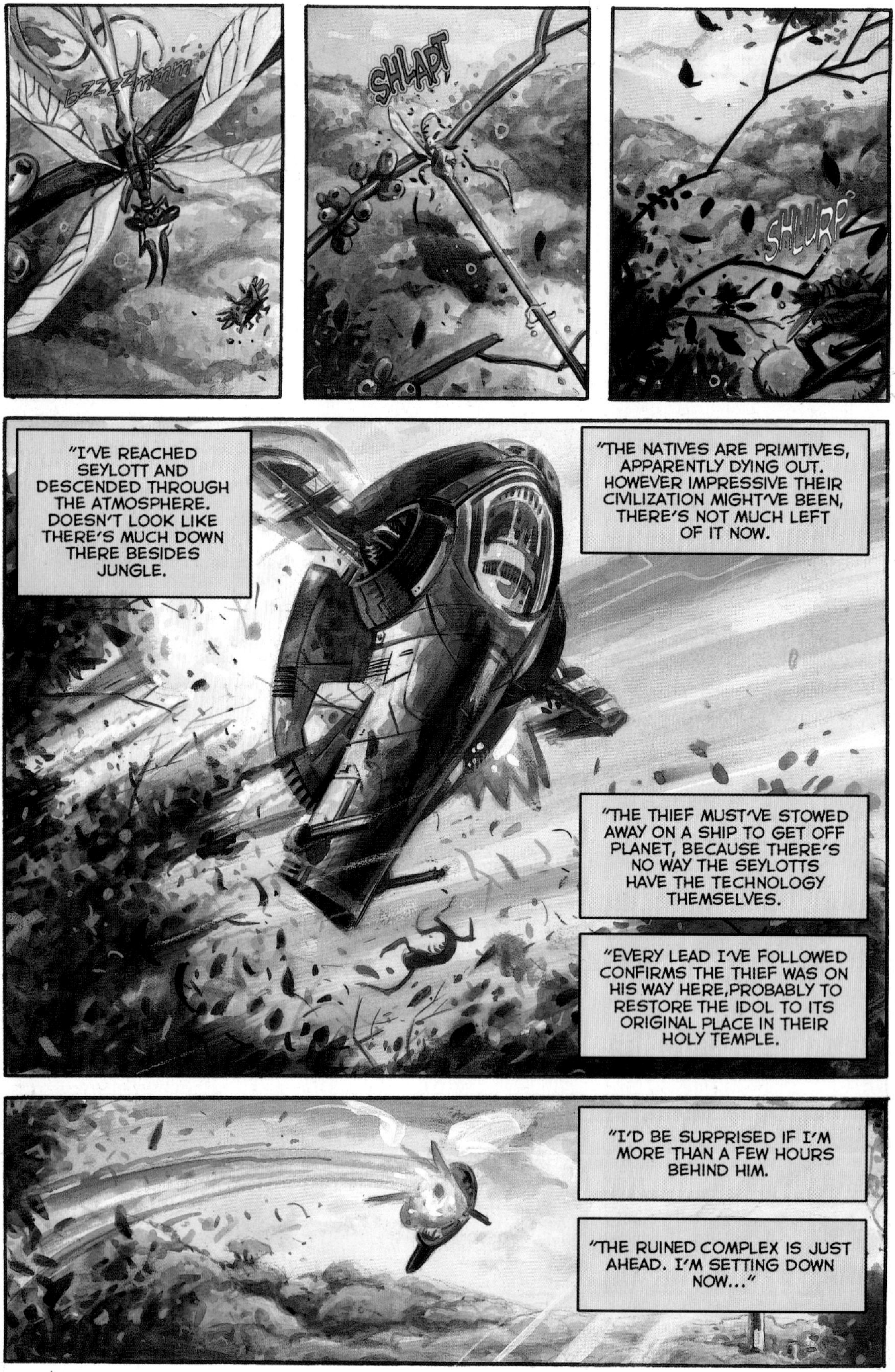
bzzzzmmm
SHLAPT
SHLURP
"I'VE REACHED SEYLOTT AND DESCENDED THROUGH THE ATMOSPHERE. DOESN'T LOOK LIKE THERE'S MUCH DOWN THERE BESIDES JUNGLE.
"THE NATIVES ARE PRIMITIVES, APPARENTLY DYING OUT. HOWEVER IMPRESSIVE THEIR CIVILIZATION MIGHT'VE BEEN, THERE'S NOT MUCH LEFT OF IT NOW.
"THE THIEF MUST'VE STOWED AWAY ON A SHIP TO GET OFF PLANET, BECAUSE THERE'S NO WAY THE SEYLOTTS HAVE THE TECHNOLOGY THEMSELVES.
"EVERY LEAD I'VE FOLLOWED CONFIRMS THE THIEF WAS ON HIS WAY HERE,PROBABLY TO RESTORE THE IDOL TO ITS ORIGINAL PLACE IN THEIR HOLY TEMPLE.
"I'D BE SURPRISED IF I'M MORE THAN A FEW HOURS BEHIND HIM.
"THE RUINED COMPLEX IS JUST AHEAD. I'M SETTING DOWN NOW..."

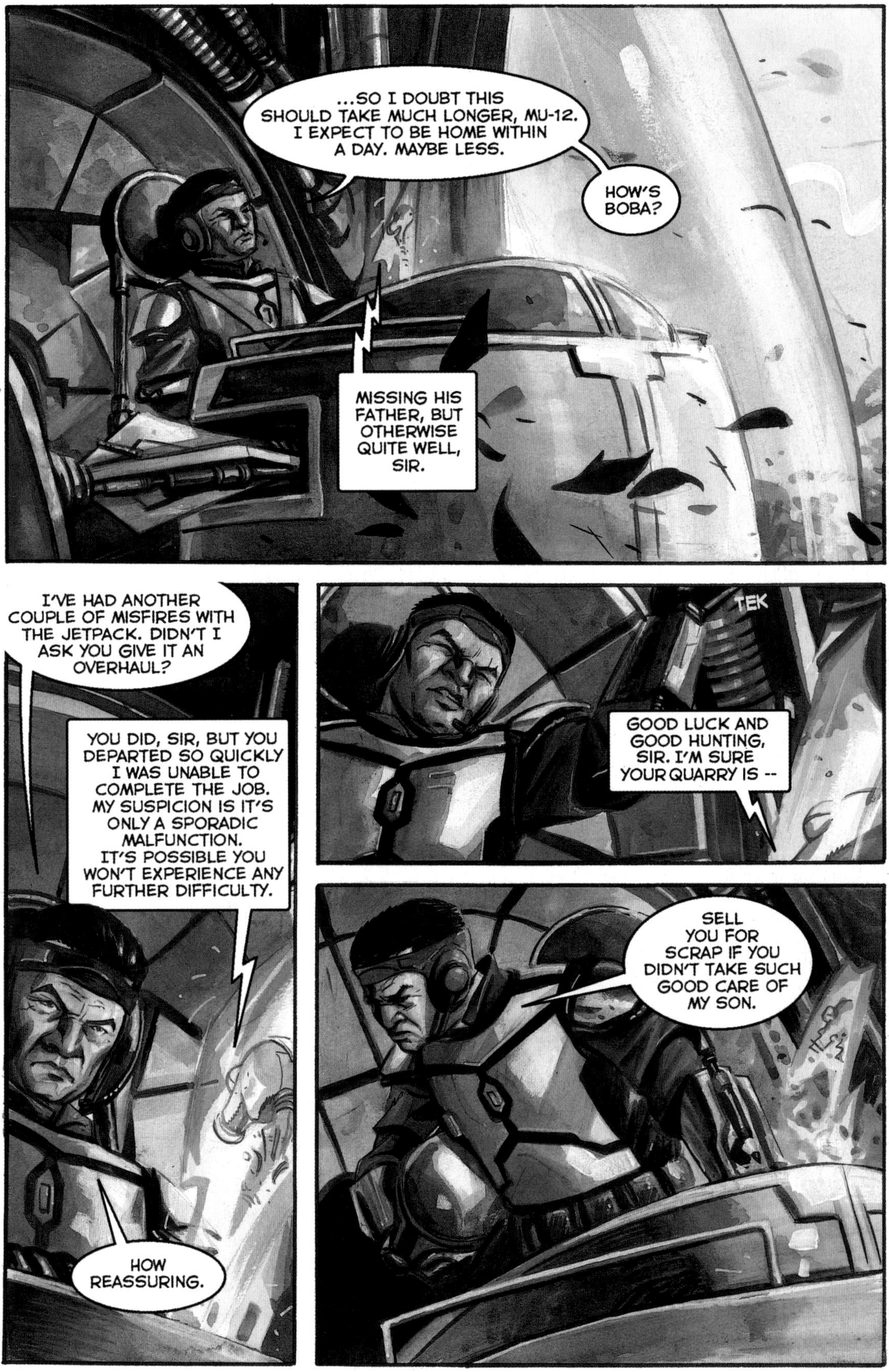
...SO I DOUBT THIS SHOULD TAKE MUCH LONGER, MU-12. I EXPECT TO BE HOME WITHIN A DAY. MAYBE LESS.
HOW'S BOBA?
MISSING HIS FATHER, BUT OTHERWISE QUITE WELL, SIR.
I'VE HAD ANOTHER COUPLE OF MISFIRES WITH THE JETPACK. DIDN'T I ASK YOU GIVE IT AN OVERHAUL?
YOU DID, SIR, BUT YOU DEPARTED SO QUICKLY I WAS UNABLE TO COMPLETE THE JOB. MY SUSPICION IS IT'S ONLY A SPORADIC MALFUNCTION. IT'S POSSIBLE YOU WON'T EXPERIENCE ANY FURTHER DIFFICULTY.
HOW REASSURING.
TEK
GOOD LUCK AND GOOD HUNTING, SIR. I'M SURE YOUR QUARRY IS --
SELL YOU FOR SCRAP IF YOU DIDN'T TAKE SUCH GOOD CARE OF MY SON.

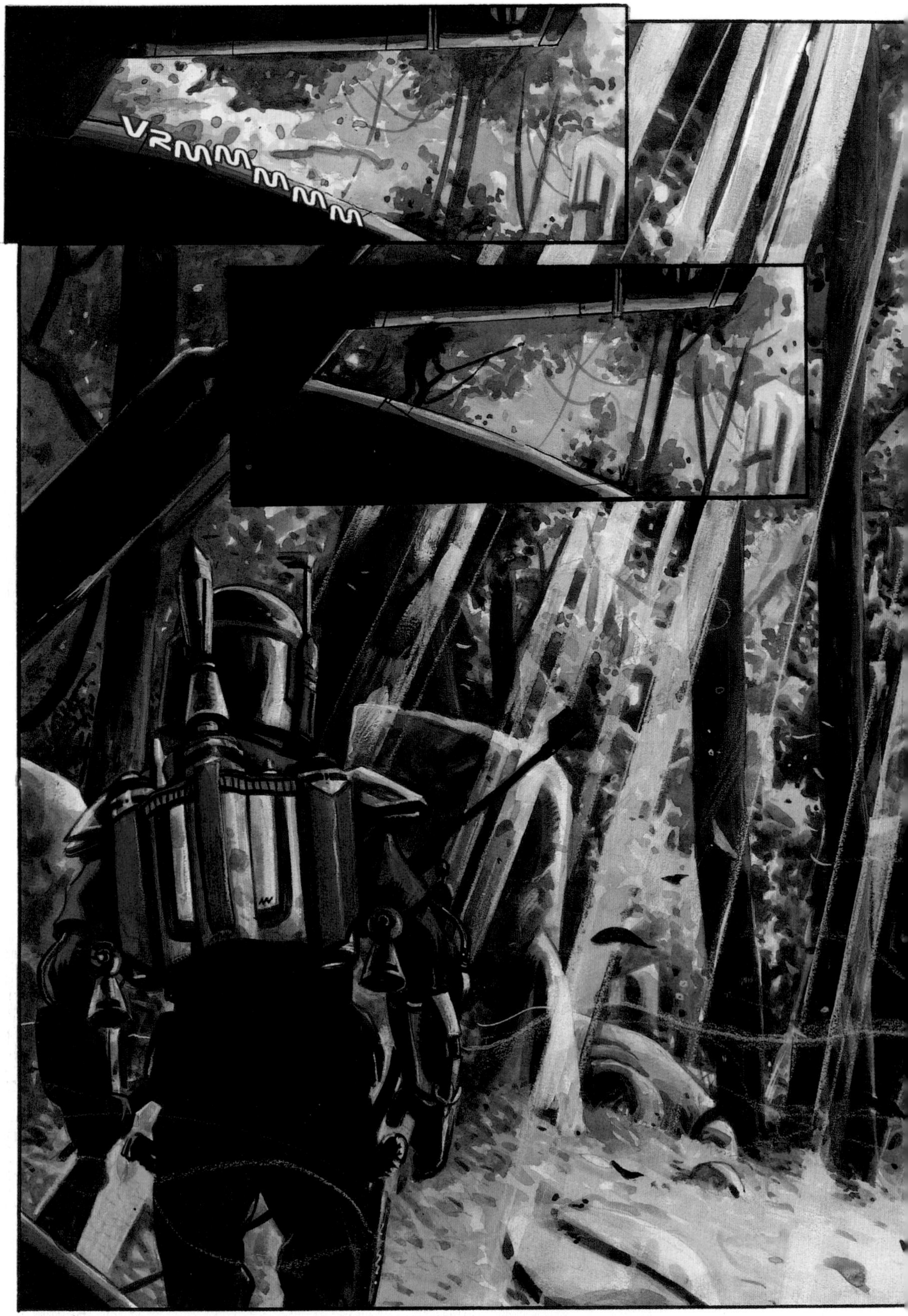
VRMMMMMMM

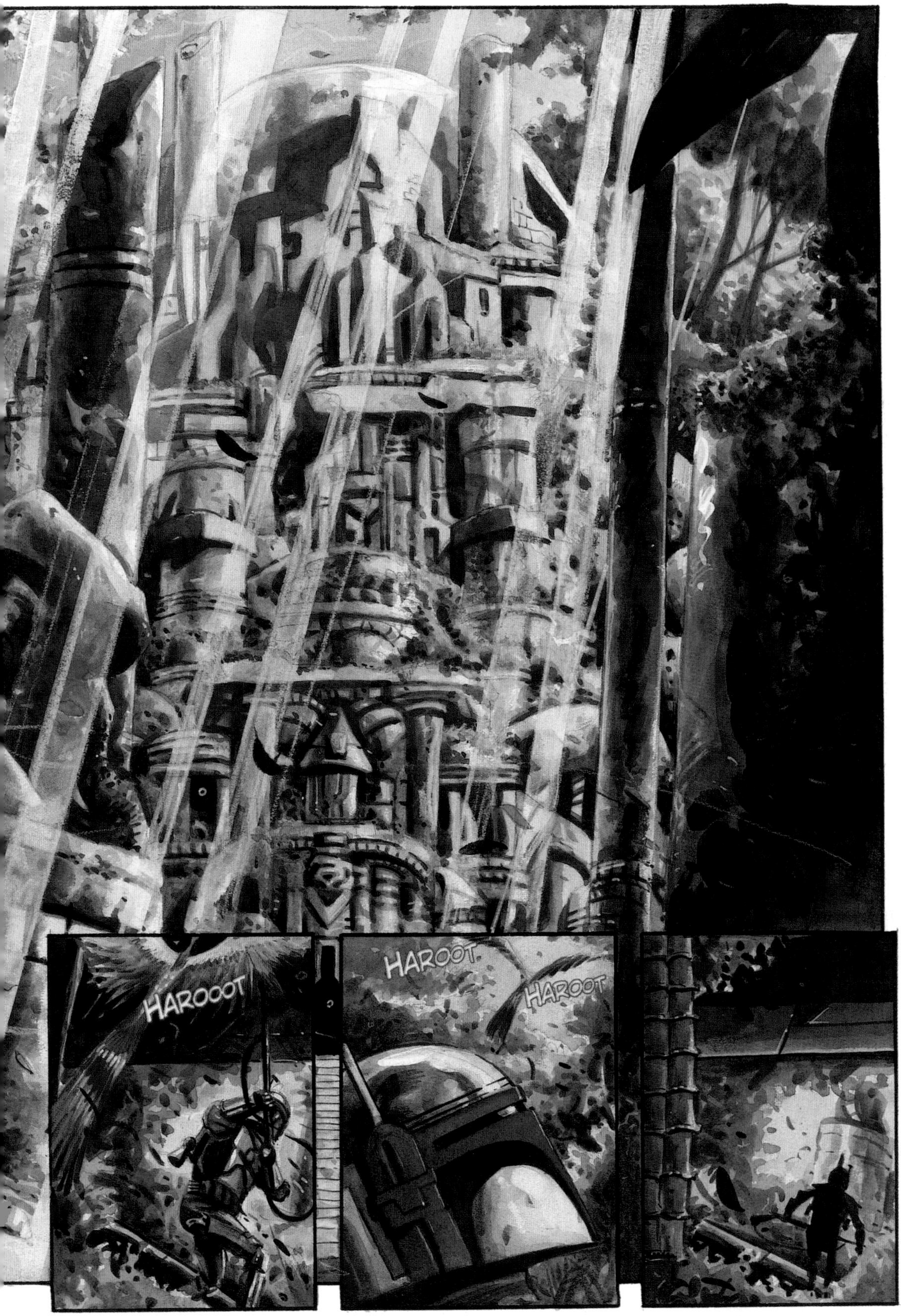
HAROOOT
HAROOT
HAROOT

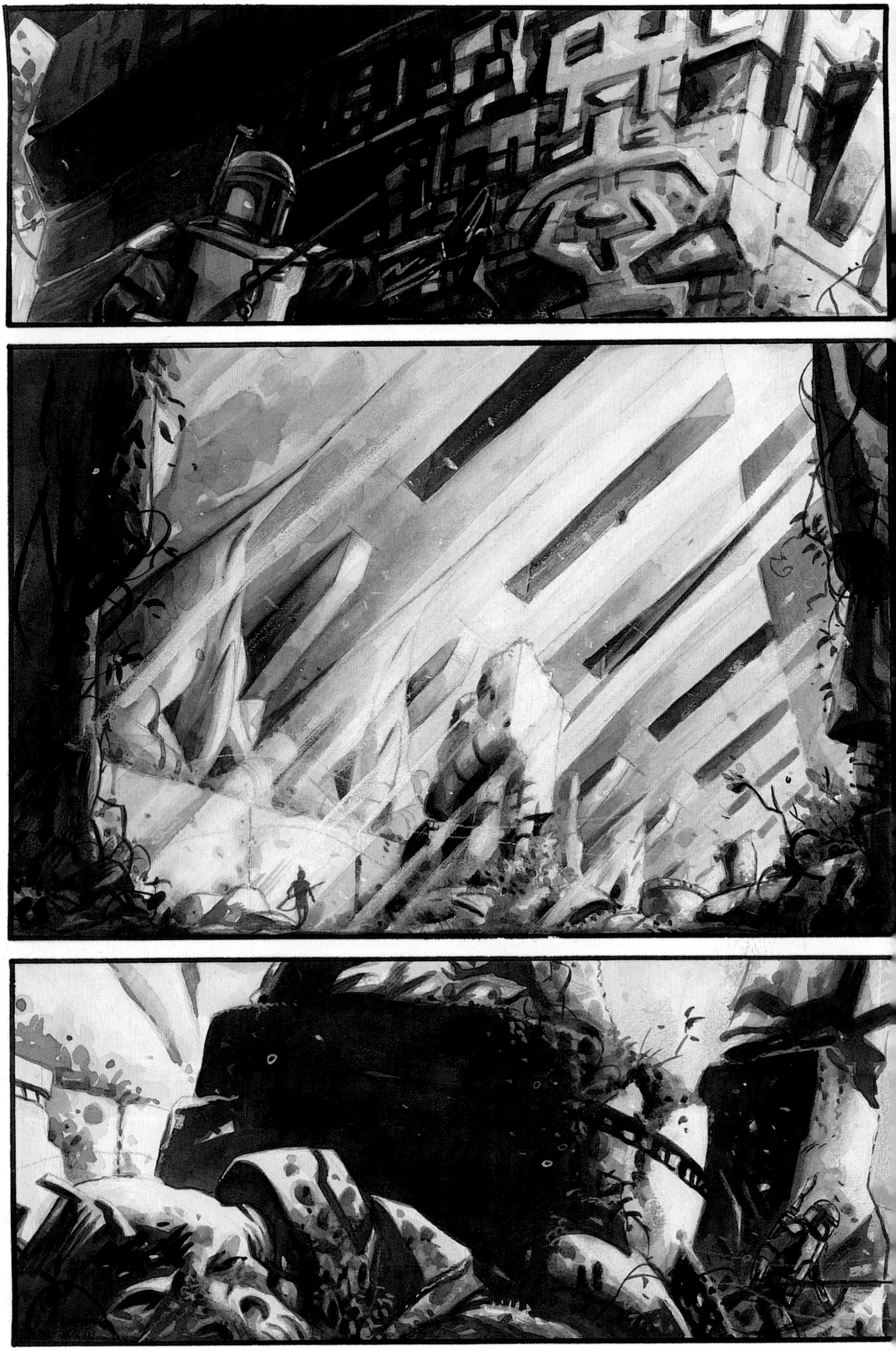

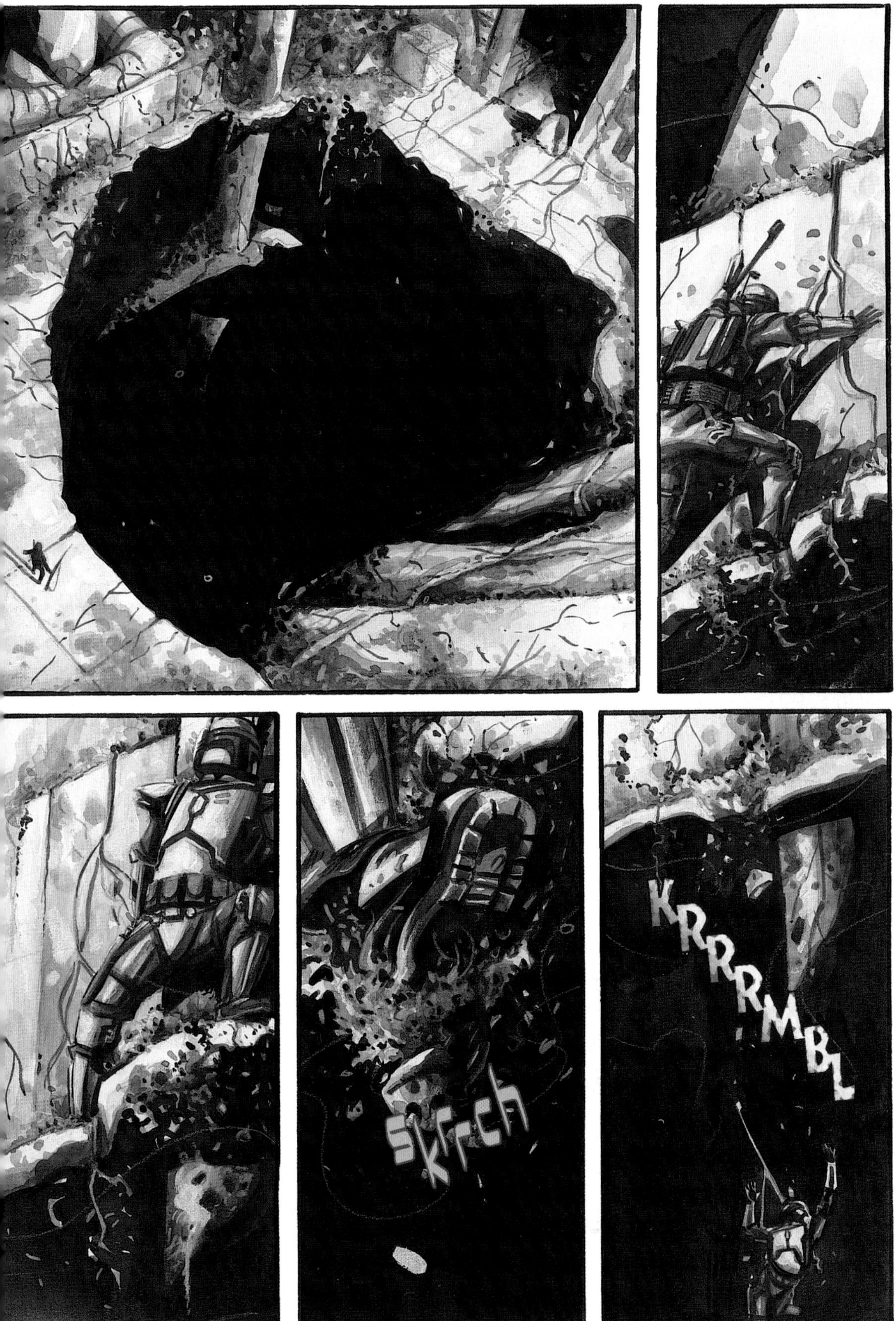
SKRRCH
KRRRMBL

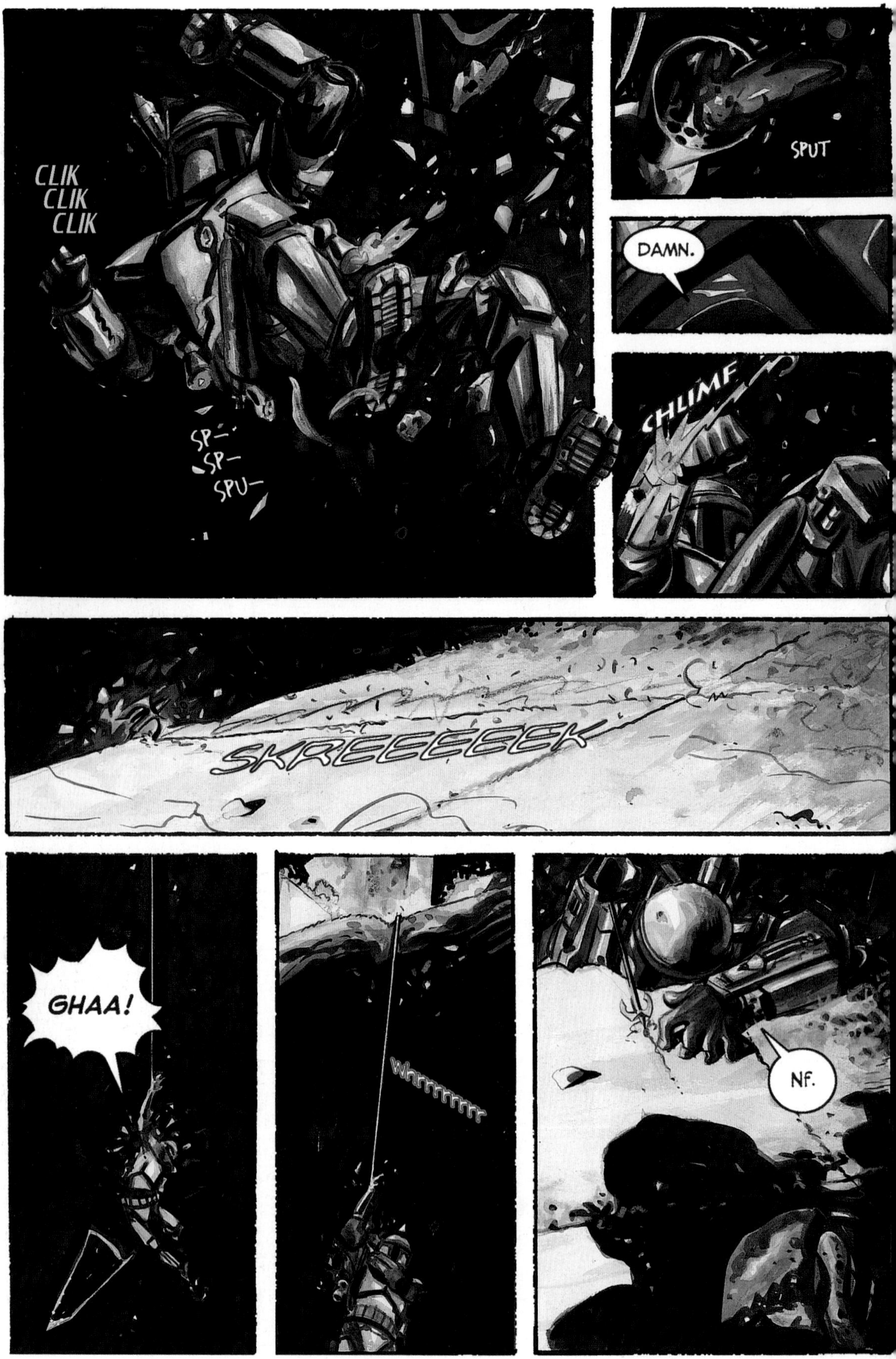
CLIK
CLIK
CLIK
SP—
SP—
SPU—
SPUT
DAMN.
CHLIMF
SKREEEEEEK
GHAA!
Whrrrrrrrrr
NF.

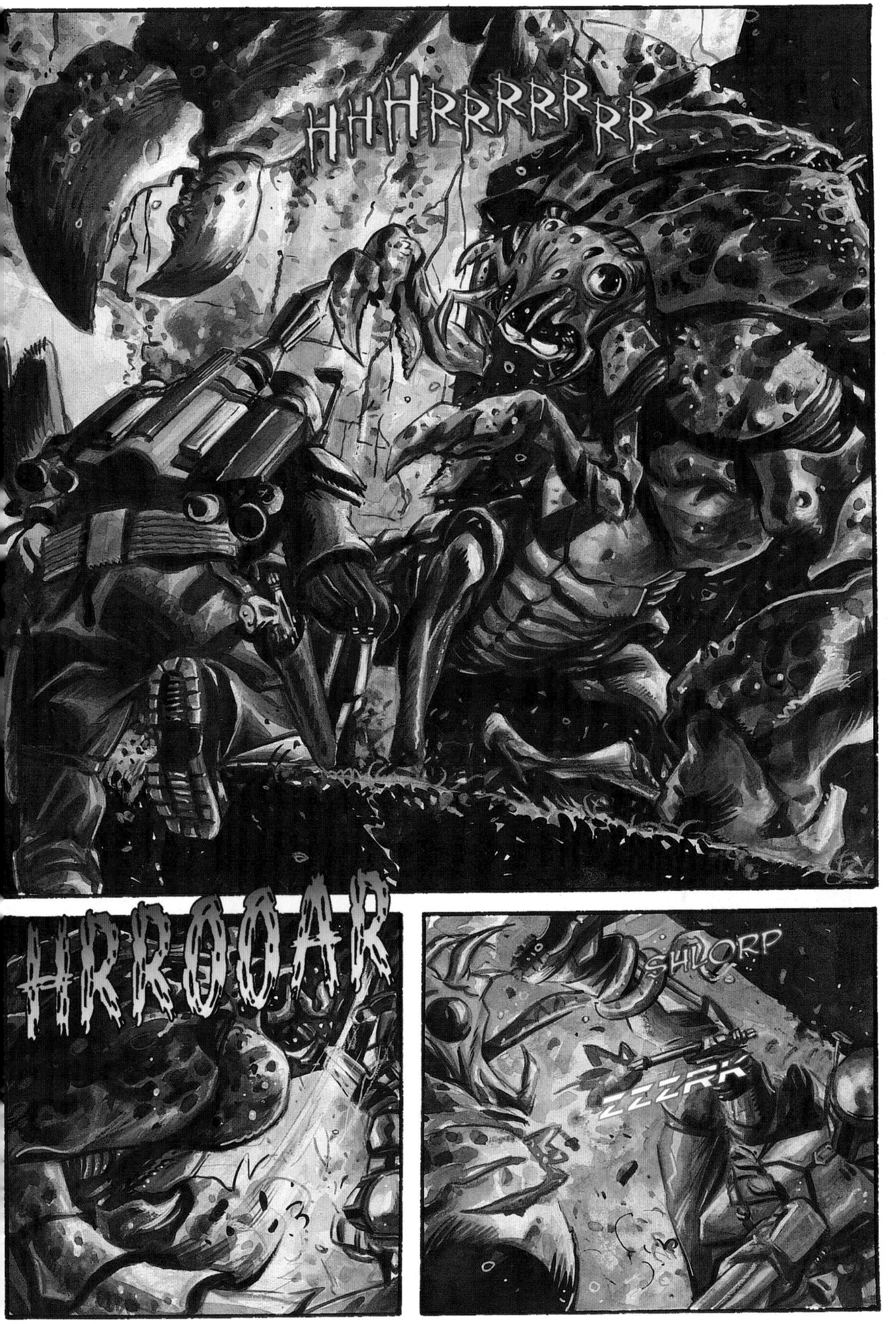
HHHRRRRRRR
HRROOAR
SHLORP
ZZZRK

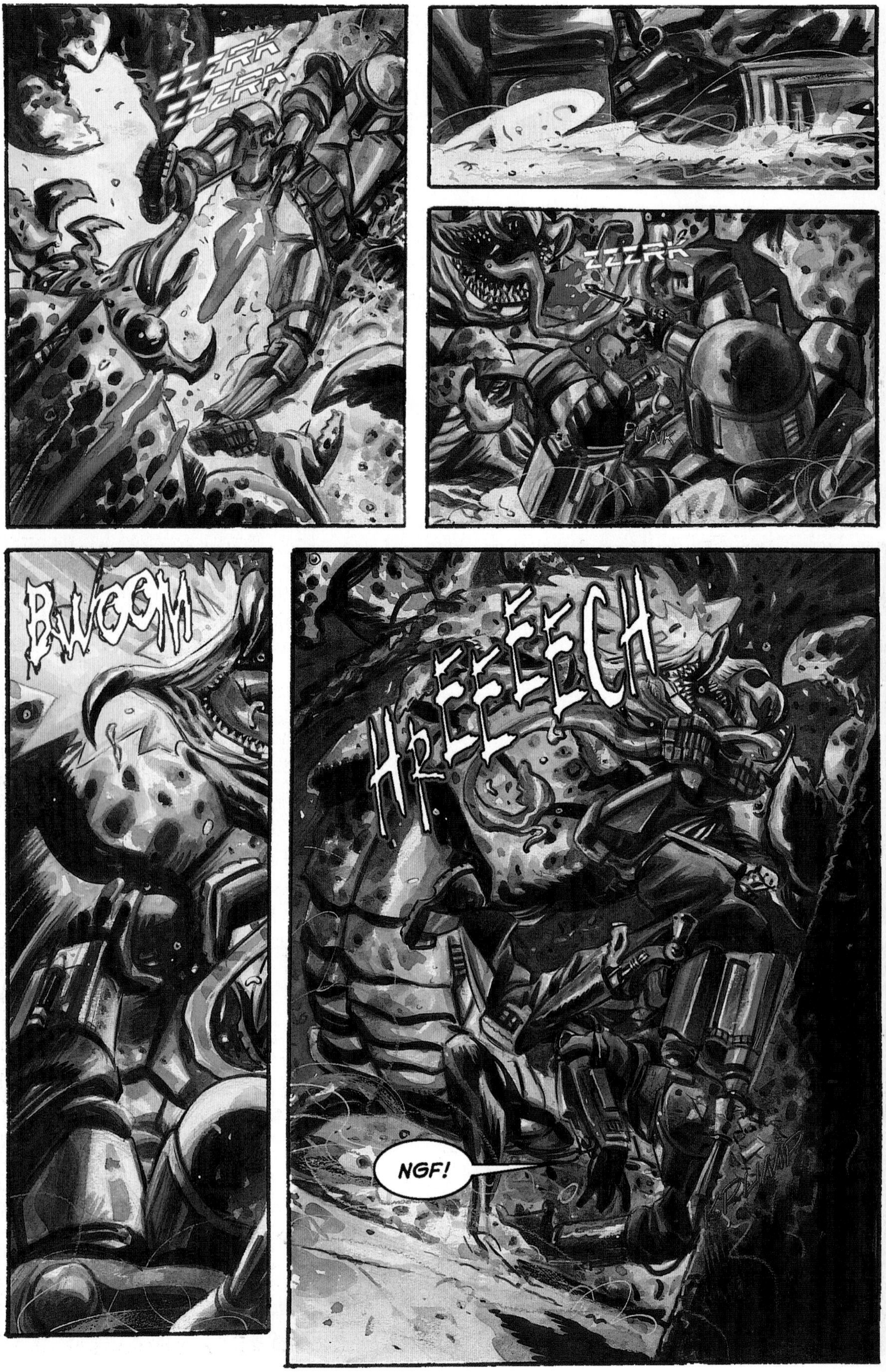
ZZZRK
ZZZRK
ZZZRK
PLINK
BWOOM
HREEEECH
NGF!

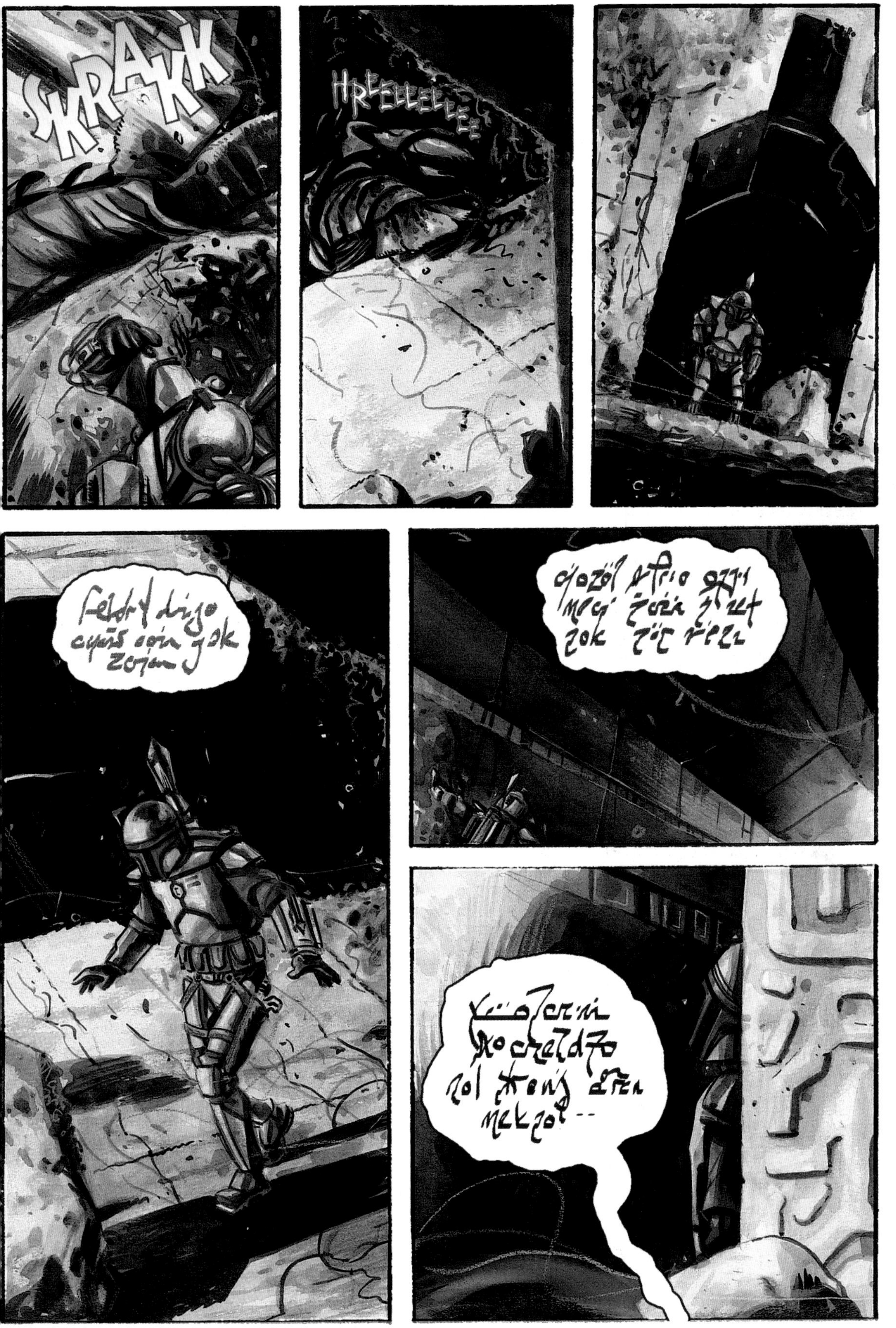
SKRAKK
HREEEEEEEEE

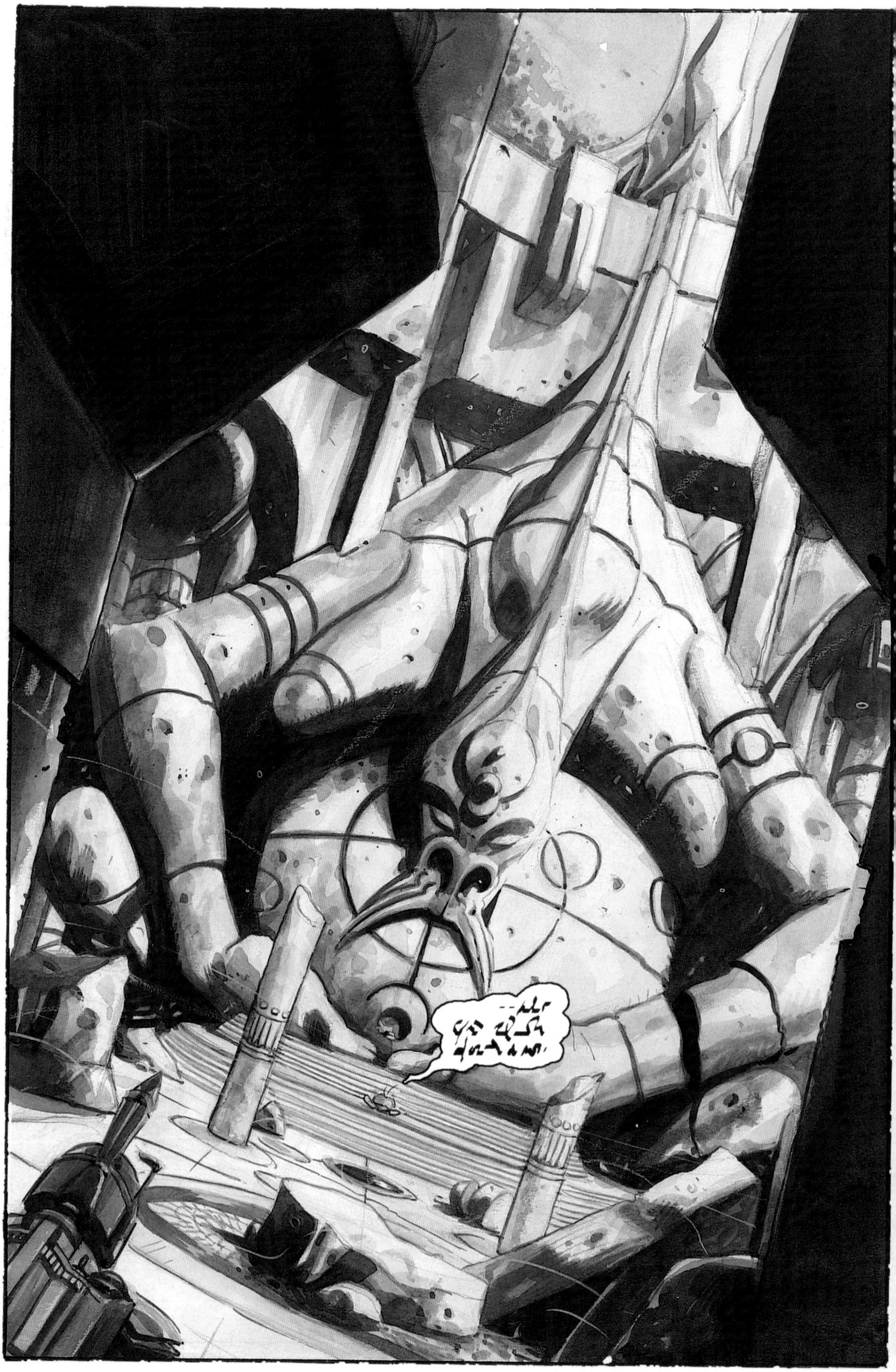

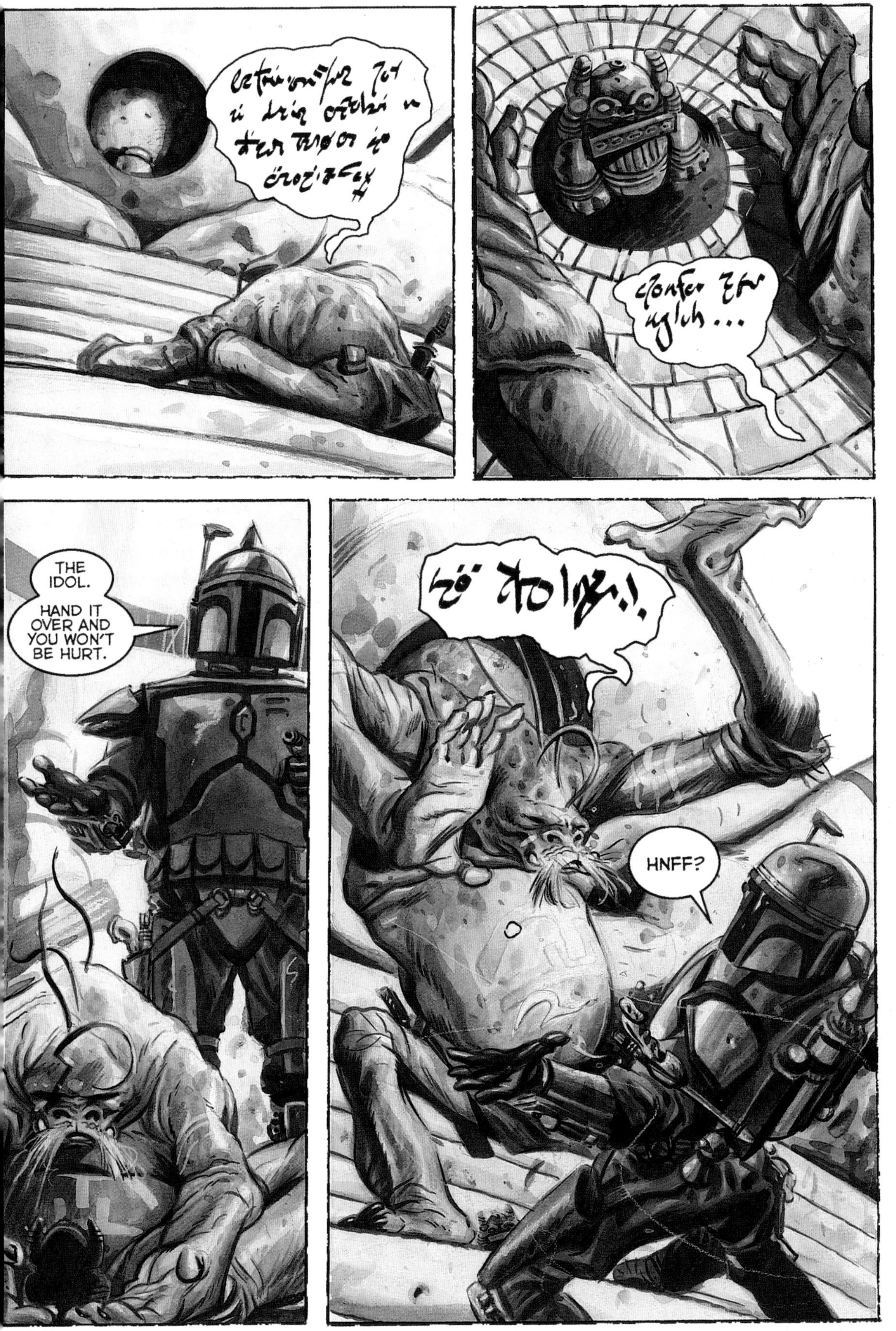
THE IDOL.
HAND IT OVER AND YOU WON'T BE HURT.
HNFF?

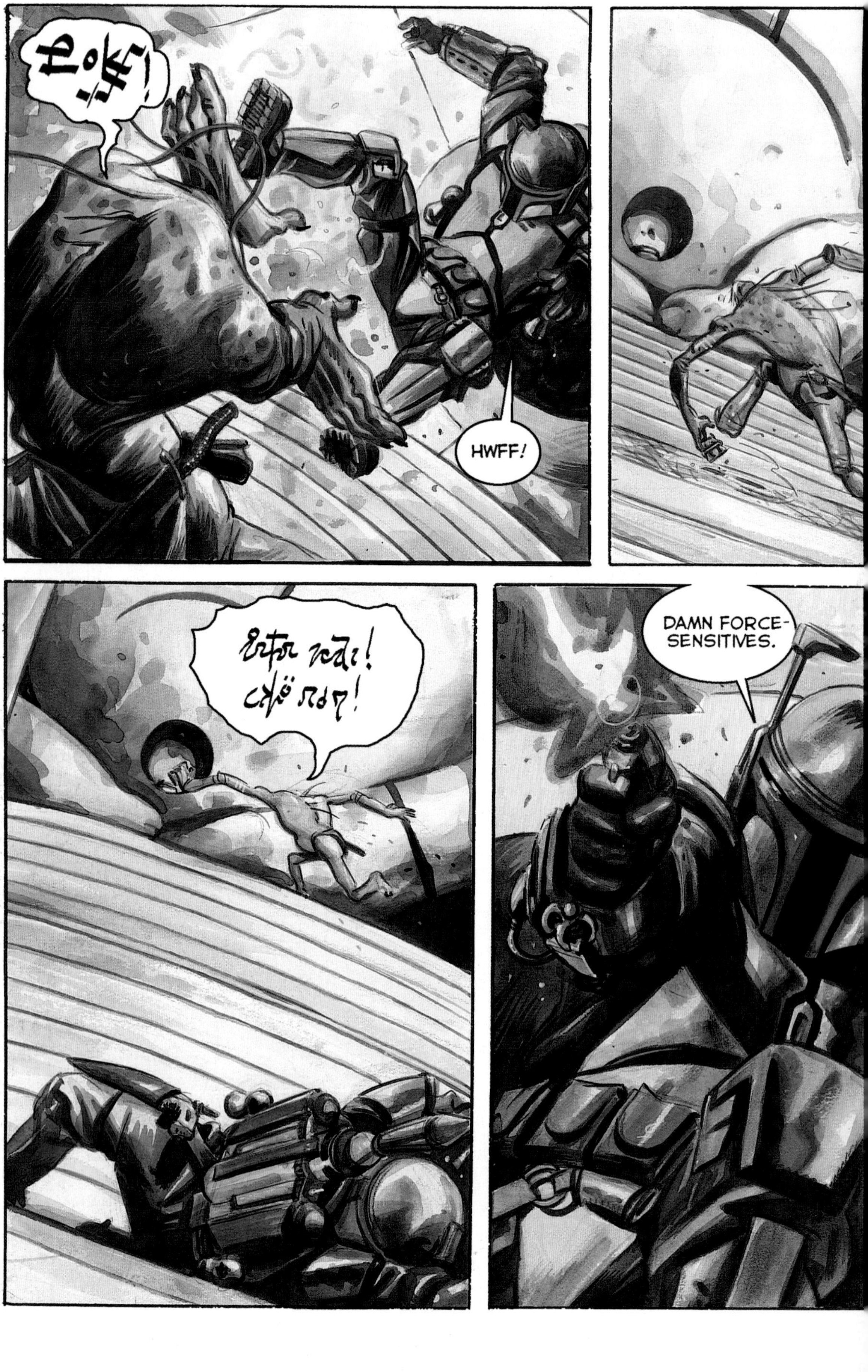
HWFF!
DAMN FORCE-SENSITIVES.

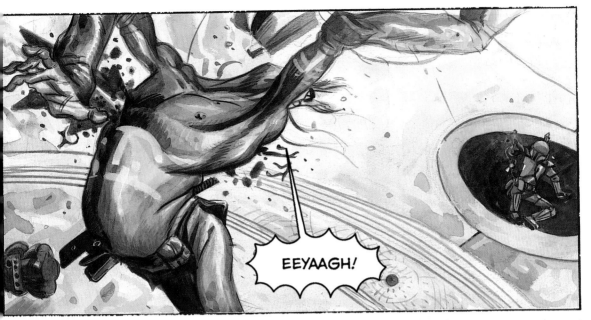

EEYAAGH!

GLLRG...

...hnngh...

...ghhh...

THIS...

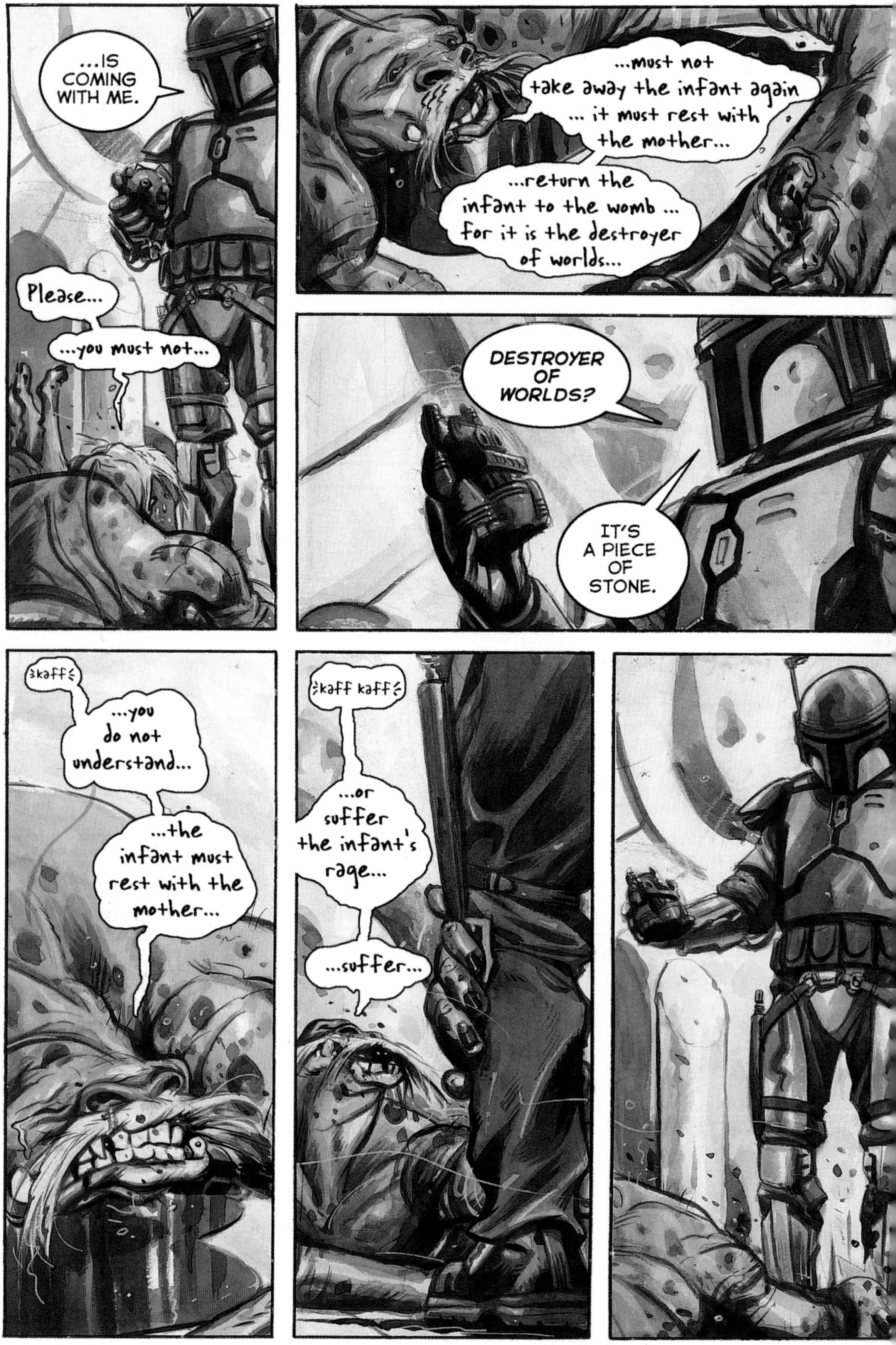

...IS COMING WITH ME.
Please...
...you must not...
...must not take away the infant again ... it must rest with the mother...
...return the infant to the womb ... for it is the destroyer of worlds...
DESTROYER OF WORLDS?
IT'S A PIECE OF STONE.
kaff
...you do not understand...
...the infant must rest with the mother...
kaff kaff
...or suffer the infant's rage...
...suffer...

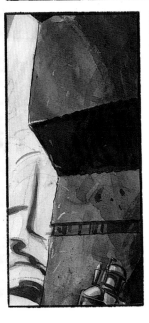

TURN AROUND, JANGO...

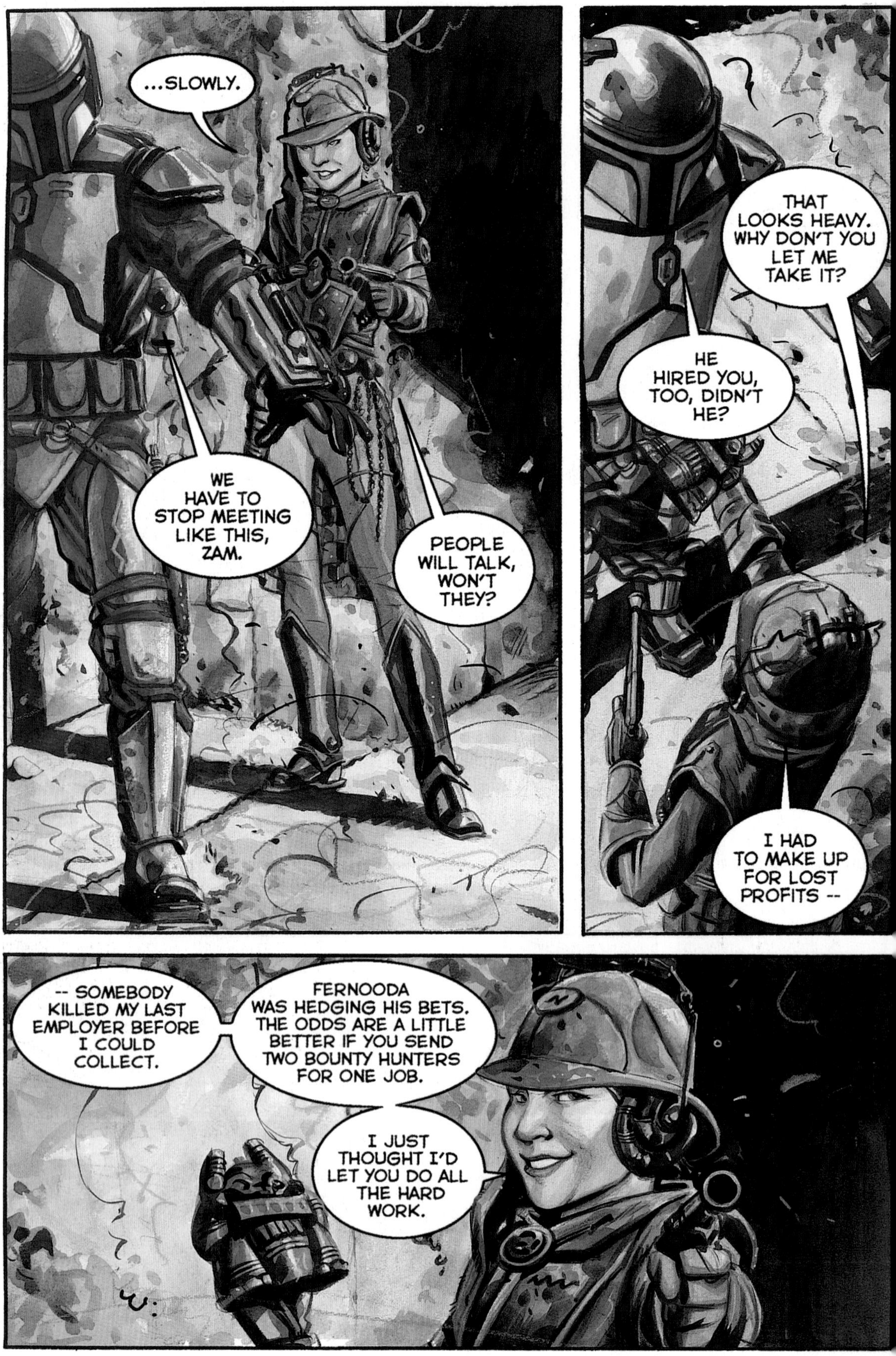
...SLOWLY.
WE HAVE TO STOP MEETING LIKE THIS, ZAM.
PEOPLE WILL TALK, WON'T THEY?
THAT LOOKS HEAVY. WHY DON'T YOU LET ME TAKE IT?
HE HIRED YOU, TOO, DIDN'T HE?
I HAD TO MAKE UP FOR LOST PROFITS --
-- SOMEBODY KILLED MY LAST EMPLOYER BEFORE I COULD COLLECT.
FERNOODA WAS HEDGING HIS BETS. THE ODDS ARE A LITTLE BETTER IF YOU SEND TWO BOUNTY HUNTERS FOR ONE JOB.
I JUST THOUGHT I'D LET YOU DO ALL THE HARD WORK.

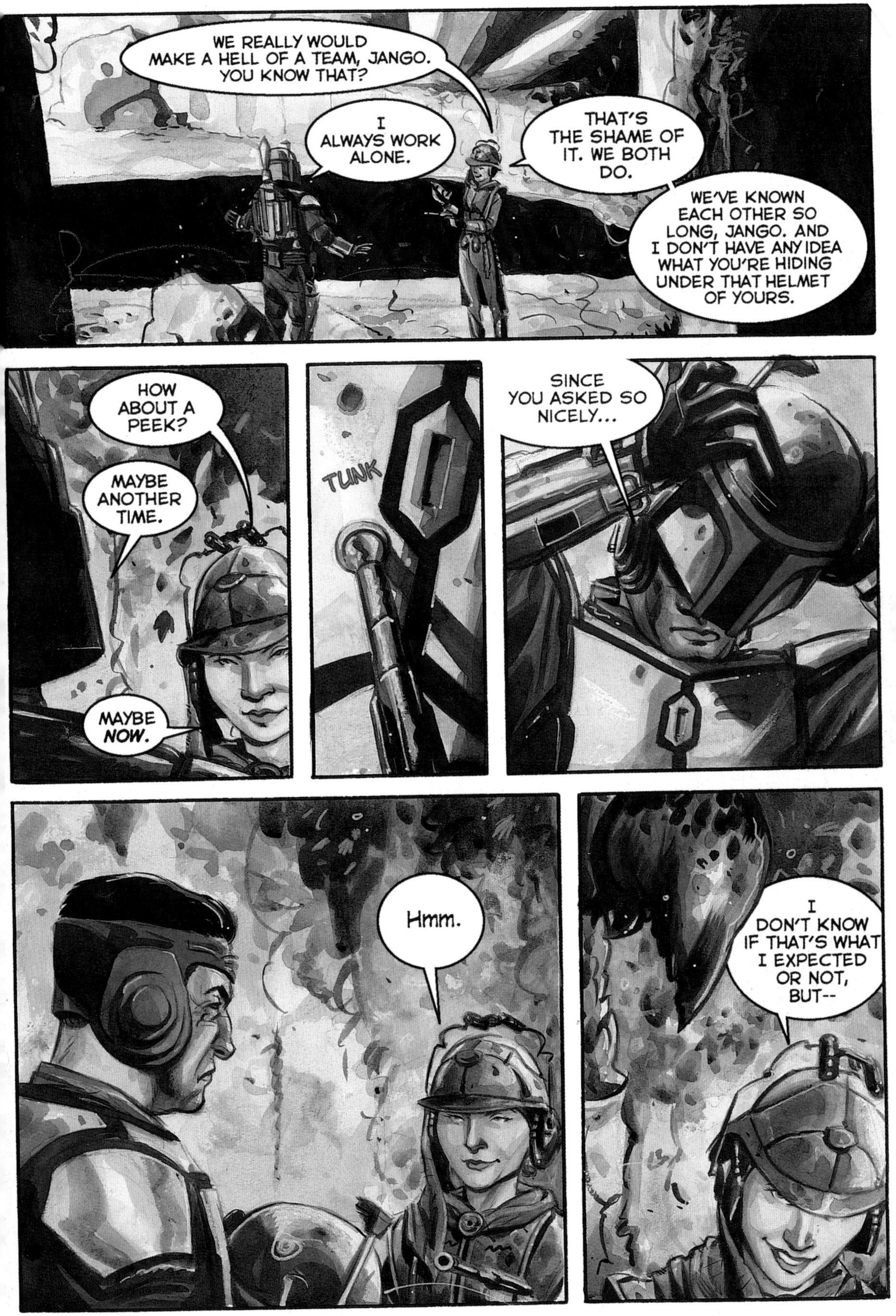
WE REALLY WOULD MAKE A HELL OF A TEAM, JANGO. YOU KNOW THAT?
I ALWAYS WORK ALONE.
THAT'S THE SHAME OF IT. WE BOTH DO.
WE'VE KNOWN EACH OTHER SO LONG, JANGO. AND I DON'T HAVE ANY IDEA WHAT YOU'RE HIDING UNDER THAT HELMET OF YOURS.
HOW ABOUT A PEEK?
MAYBE ANOTHER TIME.
MAYBE NOW.
TUNK
SINCE YOU ASKED SO NICELY...
Hmm.
I DON'T KNOW IF THAT'S WHAT I EXPECTED OR NOT, BUT--

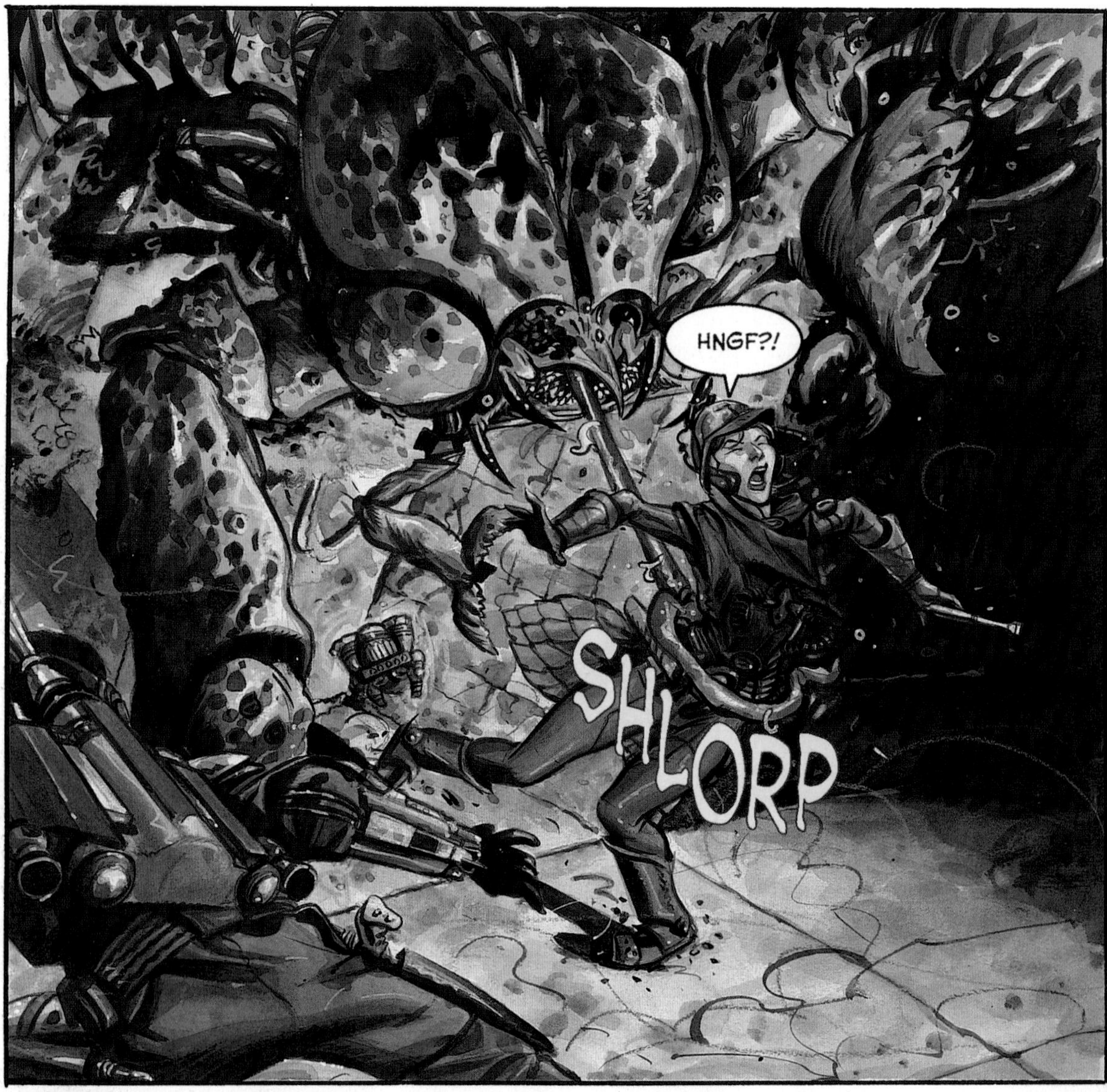
HNGF?!
SHLORP

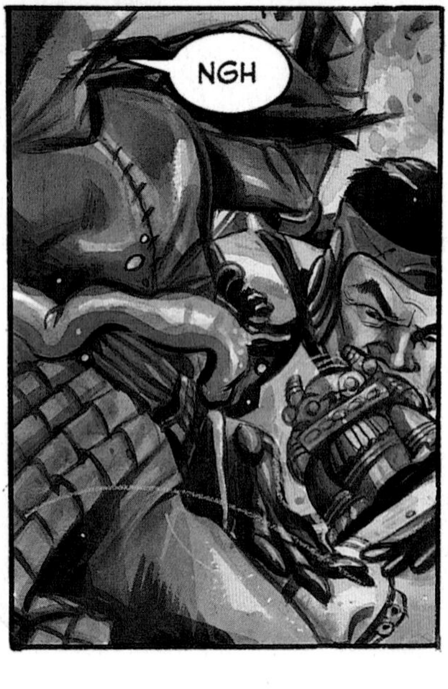
NGH

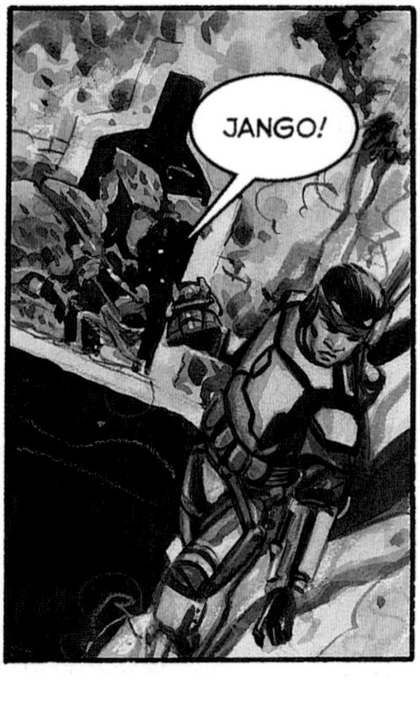
JANGO!

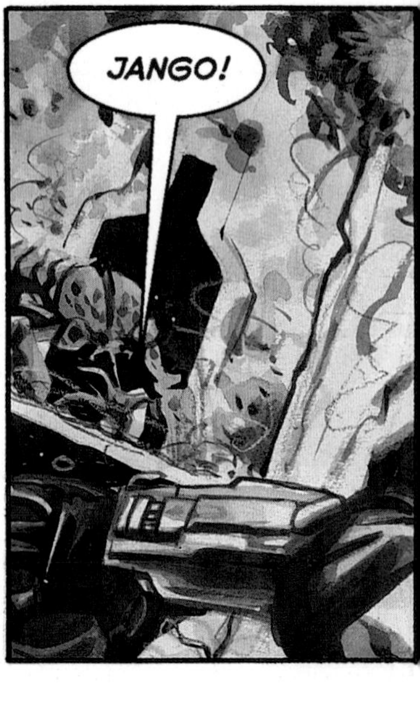
JANGO!

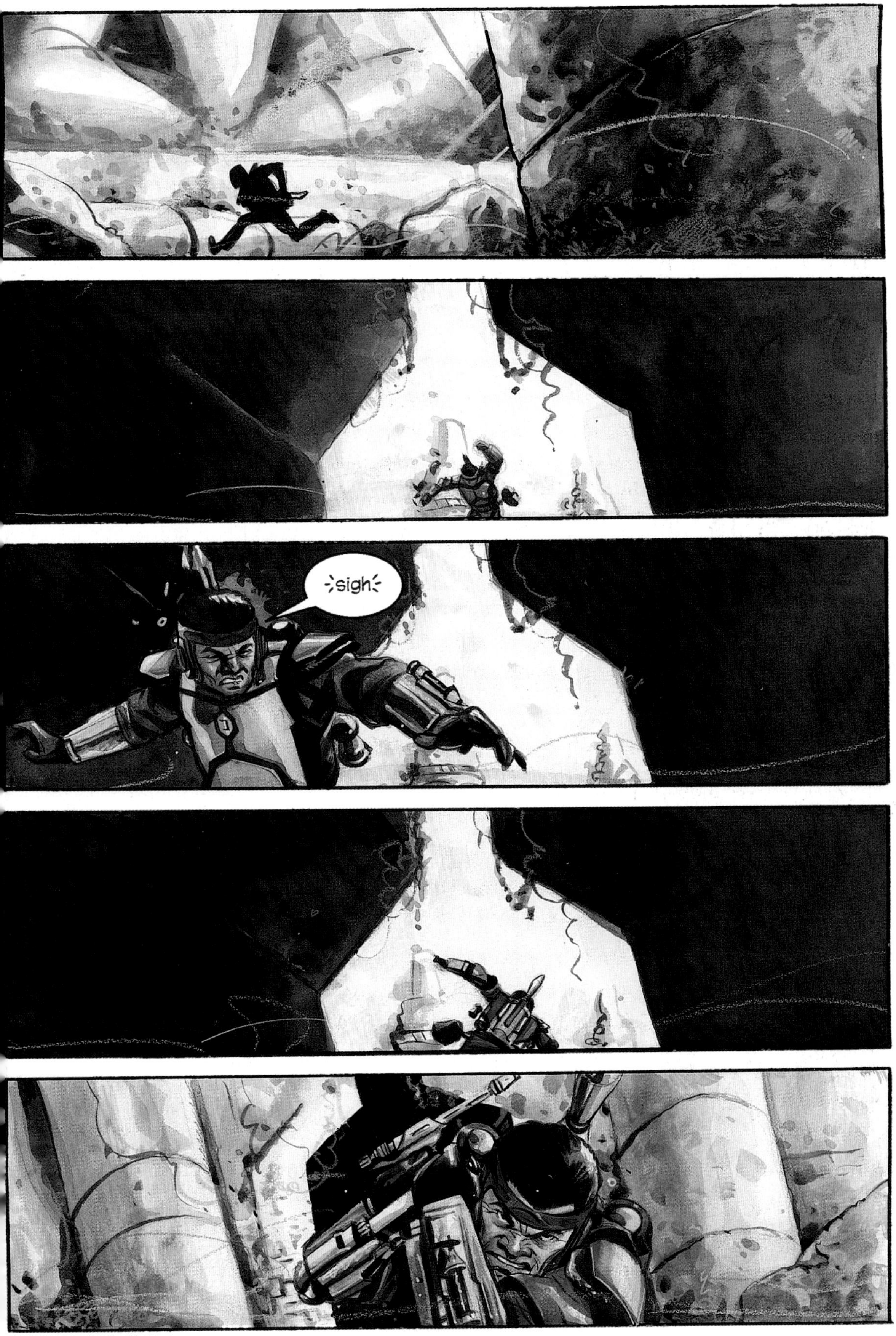
sigh

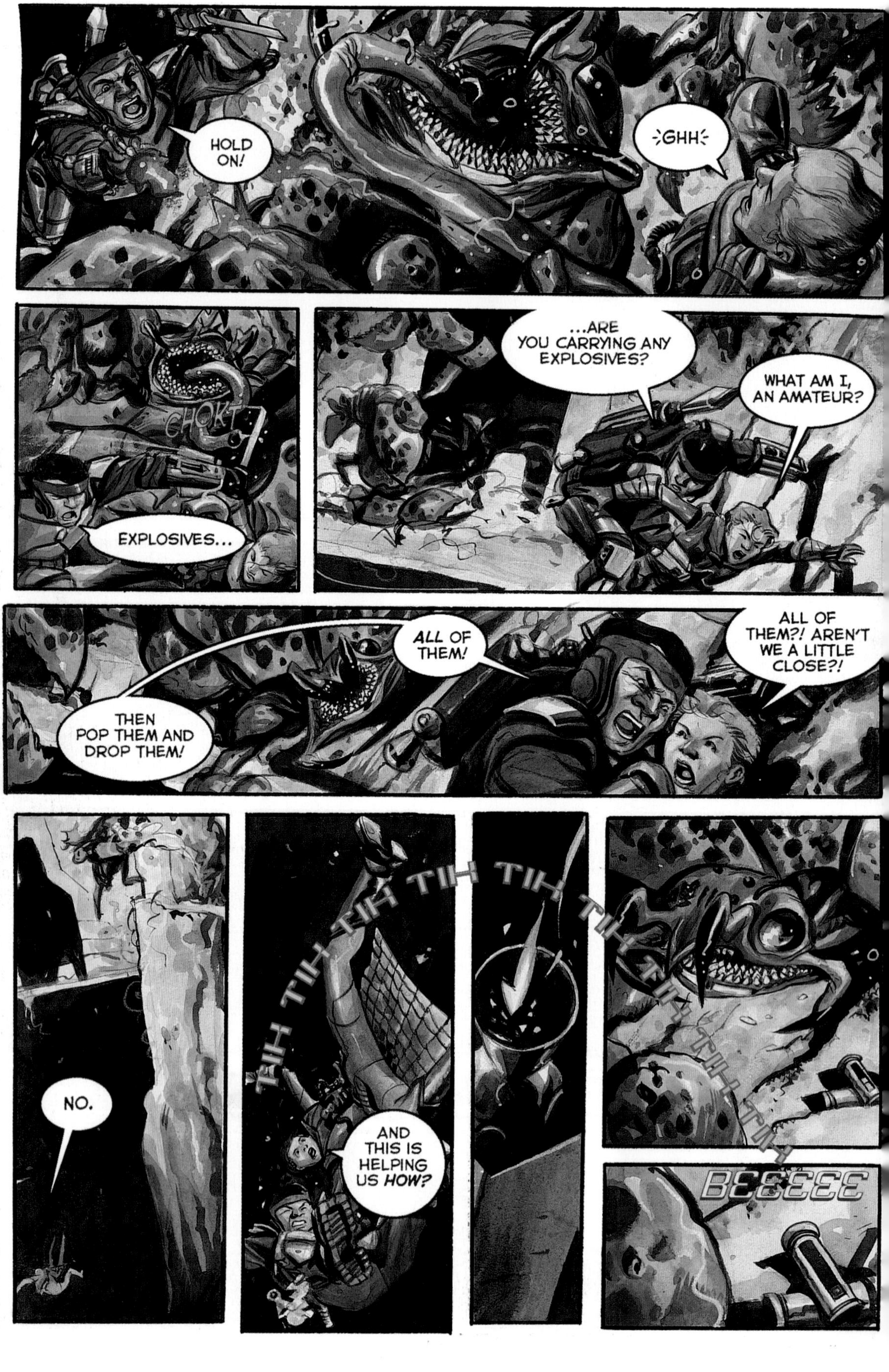
HOLD ON!
GHH
EXPLOSIVES...
...ARE YOU CARRYING ANY EXPLOSIVES?
WHAT AM I, AN AMATEUR?
ALL OF THEM?! AREN'T WE A LITTLE CLOSE?!
ALL OF THEM!
THEN POP THEM AND DROP THEM!
NO.
AND THIS IS HELPING US HOW?
TIH TIH TIH TIH TIH TIH TIH TIH TIH
BEEEEE

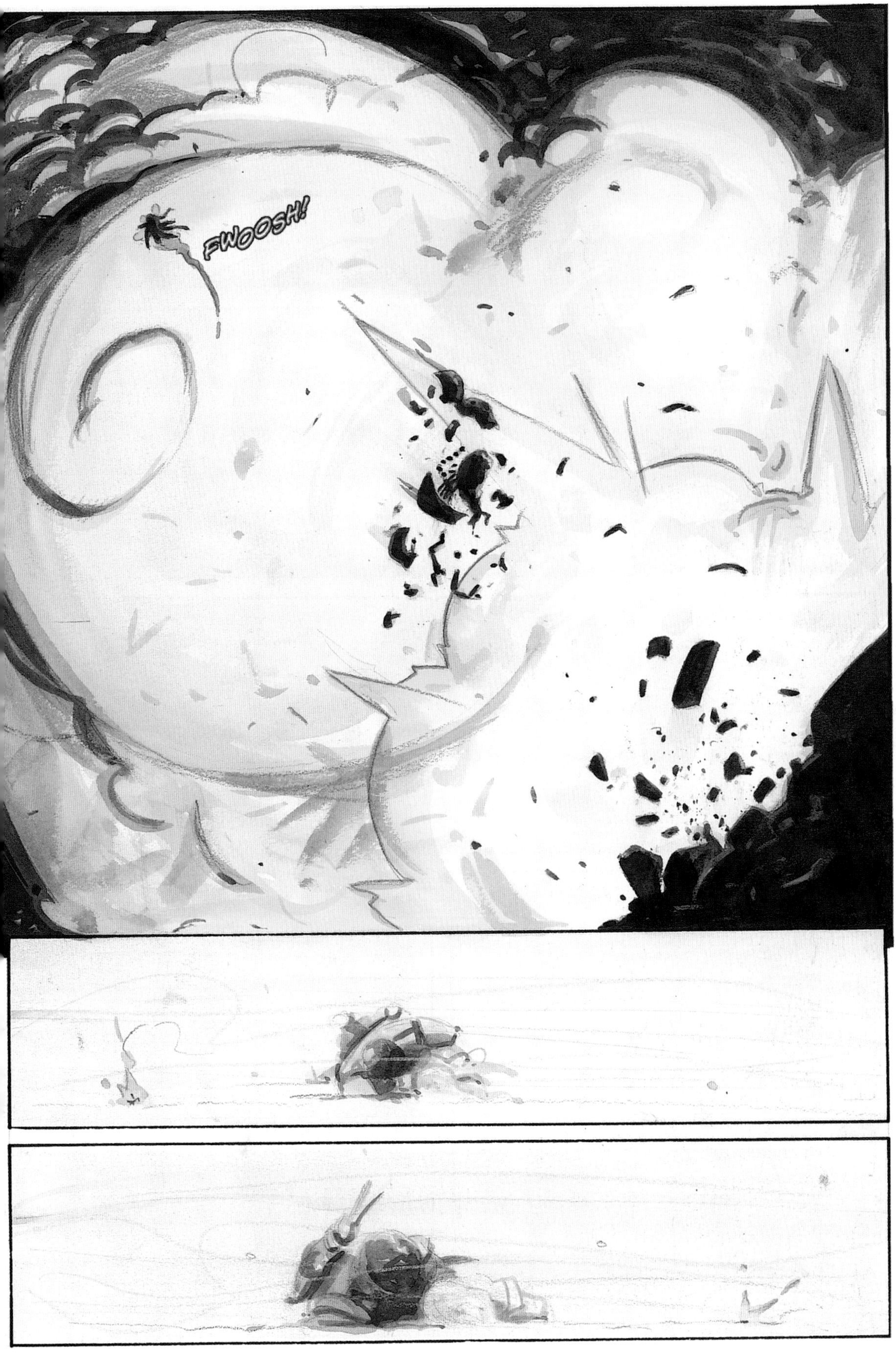
FWOOSH!

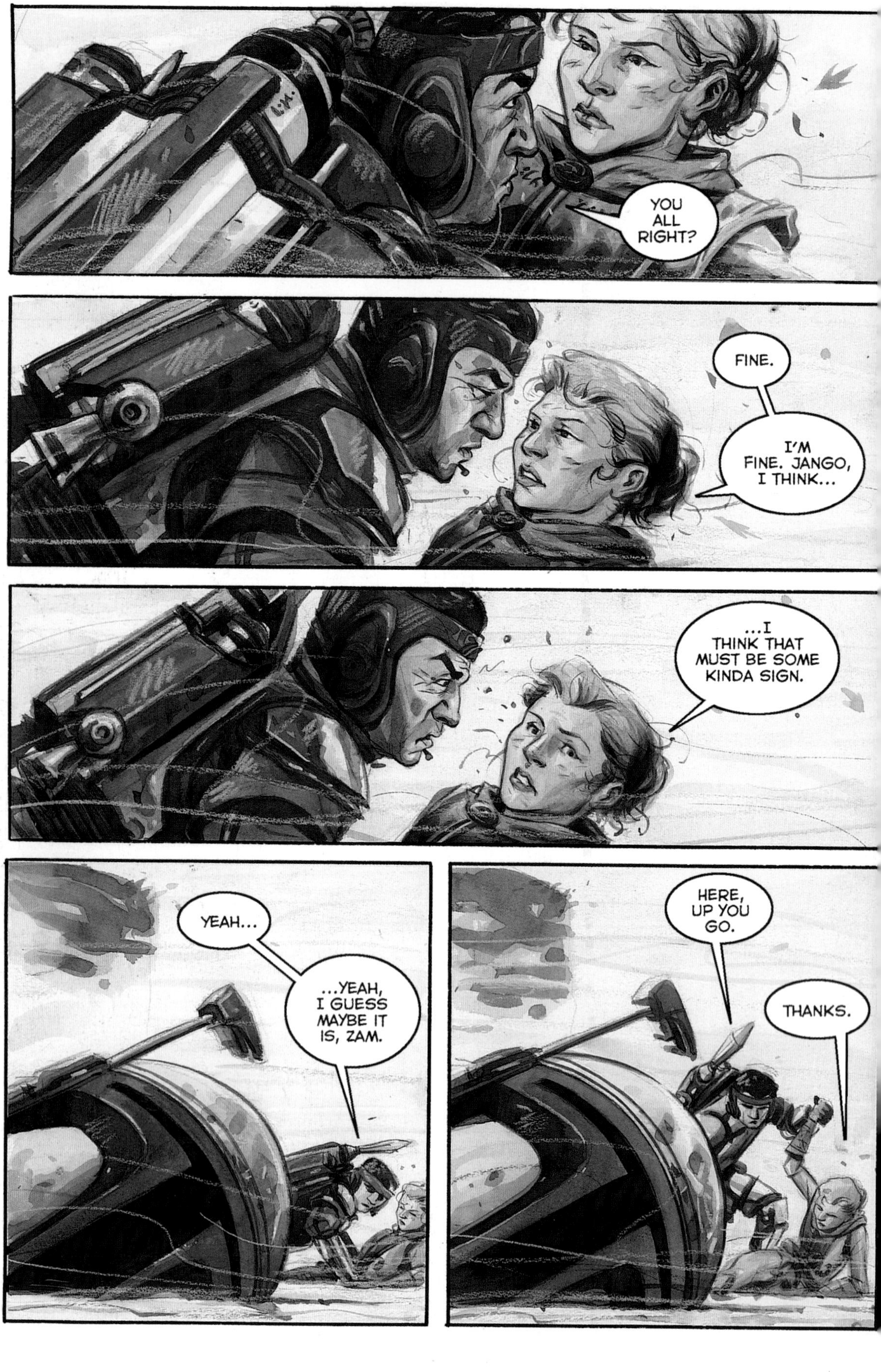
YOU ALL RIGHT?
FINE.
I'M FINE. JANGO, I THINK...
...I THINK THAT MUST BE SOME KINDA SIGN.
YEAH...
...YEAH, I GUESS MAYBE IT IS, ZAM.
HERE, UP YOU GO.
THANKS.

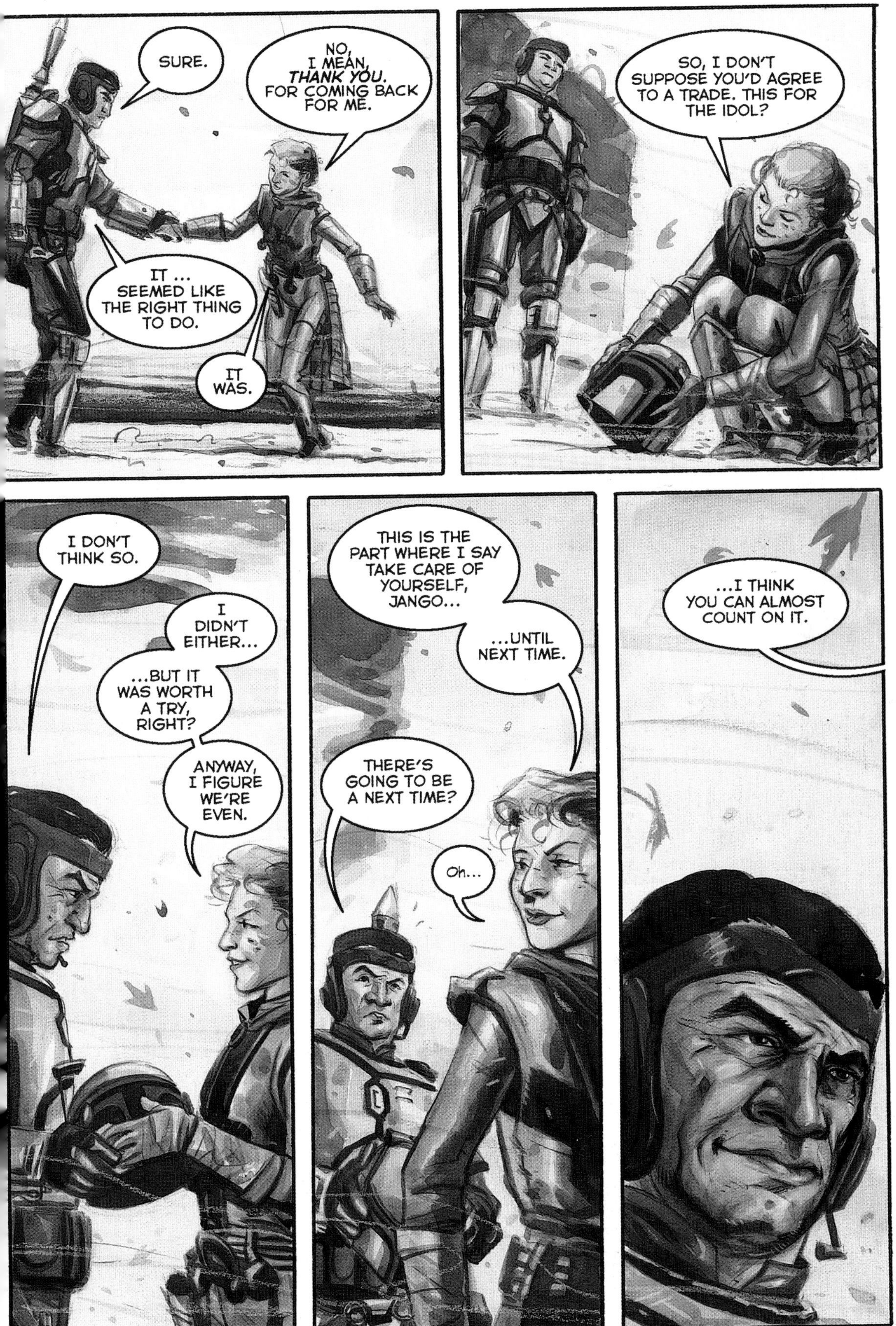
SURE.
NO, I MEAN, *THANK YOU.* FOR COMING BACK FOR ME.
IT ... SEEMED LIKE THE RIGHT THING TO DO.
IT WAS.
SO, I DON'T SUPPOSE YOU'D AGREE TO A TRADE. THIS FOR THE IDOL?
I DON'T THINK SO.
I DIDN'T EITHER...
...BUT IT WAS WORTH A TRY, RIGHT?
ANYWAY, I FIGURE WE'RE EVEN.
THIS IS THE PART WHERE I SAY TAKE CARE OF YOURSELF, JANGO...
...UNTIL NEXT TIME.
THERE'S GOING TO BE A NEXT TIME?
Oh...
...I THINK YOU CAN ALMOST COUNT ON IT.

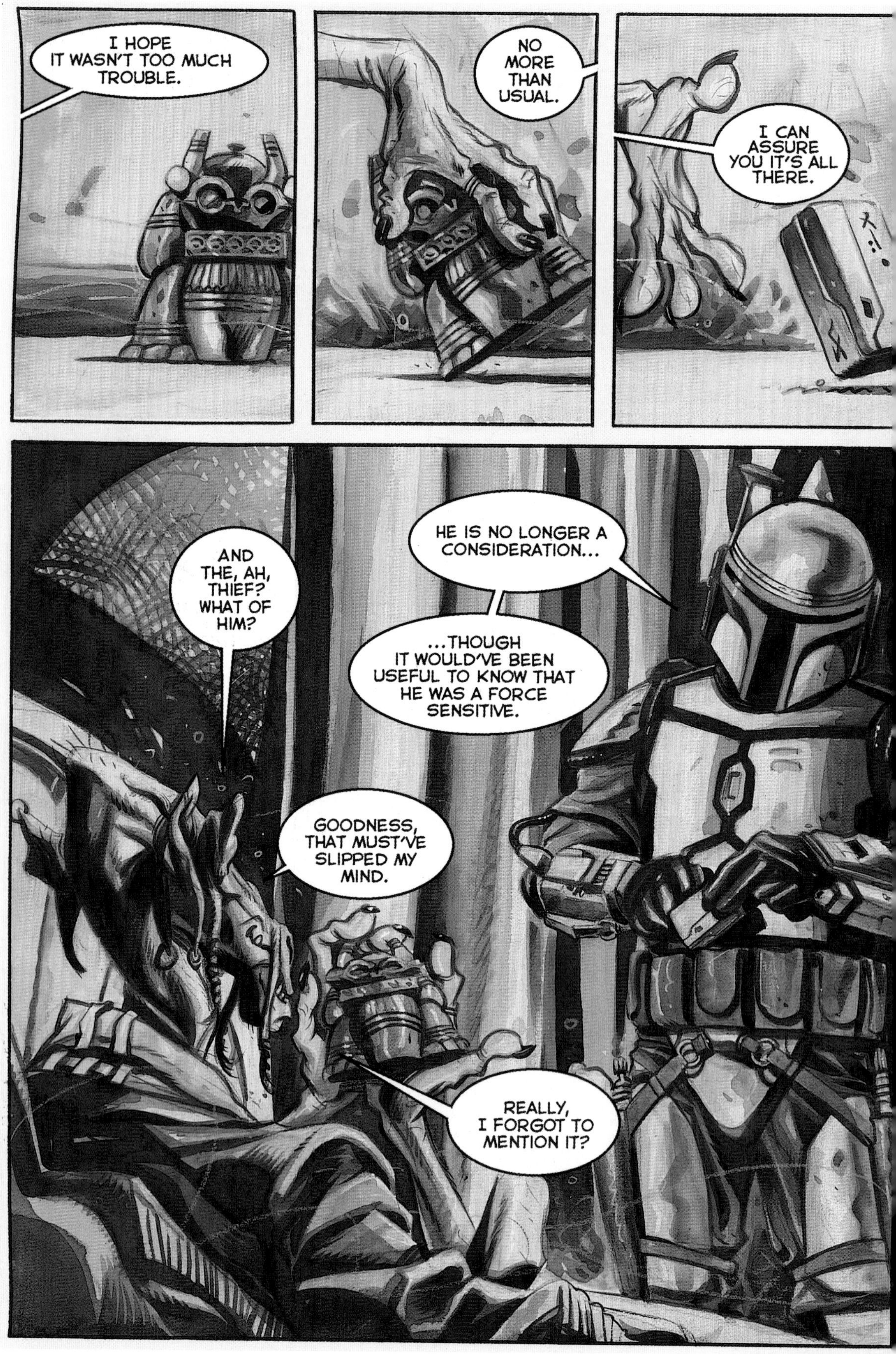
I HOPE IT WASN'T TOO MUCH TROUBLE.
NO MORE THAN USUAL.
I CAN ASSURE YOU IT'S ALL THERE.
AND THE, AH, THIEF? WHAT OF HIM?
HE IS NO LONGER A CONSIDERATION...
...THOUGH IT WOULD'VE BEEN USEFUL TO KNOW THAT HE WAS A FORCE SENSITIVE.
GOODNESS, THAT MUST'VE SLIPPED MY MIND.
REALLY, I FORGOT TO MENTION IT?

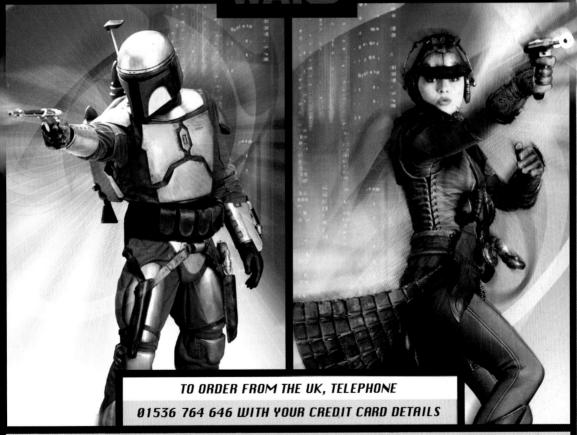

OTHER TITLES AVAILABLE FROM TITAN BOOKS

ANGEL

AUTUMNAL
Golden • Sniegoski • Zanier
80 page colour paperback
ISBN: 1-84023-396-6

EARTHLY POSSESSIONS
Golden • Sniegoski • Zanier
96 page colour paperback
ISBN: 1-84023-280-3

THE HOLLOWER
Golden • Gomez • Florea
88-page colour paperback
ISBN: 1-84023-163-7

HUNTING GROUND
Golden • Sniegoski • Powell
96 page colour paperback
ISBN: 1-84023-338-9

SURROGATES
Golden •Zanier •
Owens • Gomez
80-page colour paperback
ISBN: 1-84023-234-X

BUFFY THE VAMPIRE SLAYER

AUTUMNAL
Boal • Fassbender • Pascoe •
Richards • Pimentel
80 page colour paperback
ISBN: 1-84023-382-6

BAD BLOOD
Watson • Bennett • Ketcham
88-page colour paperback
ISBN: 1-84023-179-3

THE BLOOD OF CARTHAGE
Golden • Richards • Pimentel
128-page colour paperback
ISBN: 1-84023-281-1

CRASH TEST DEMONS
Watson • Richards • Pimentel
88-page colour paperback
ISBN: 1-84023-199-8

CREATURES OF HABIT
Fassbender • Pascoe •
Horton • Lee
128 page colour paperback
ISBN: 1-84023-426-1

THE DUST WALTZ
Brereton • Gomez
80-page colour paperback
ISBN: 1-84023-057-6

FOOD CHAIN
Petrie • Golden •
Richards • Zanier
168 page colour paperback
ISBN: 1-84023-315-X

THE ORIGIN
Golden • Brereton •
Bennett • Ketcham
80-page colour paperback
ISBN: 1-84023-105-X

PALE REFLECTIONS
Watson • Richards • Pimentel
96-page colour paperback
ISBN: 1-84023-236-6

PAST LIVES
Golden • Sniegoski •
Zanier • Richards
168 page colour paperback
ISBN: 1-84023-366-4

THE REMAINING SUNLIGHT
Watson • Van Meter •
Bennett • Ross
88-page colour paperback
ISBN: 1-84023-078-9

RING OF FIRE
Petrie • Sook
80-page colour paperback
ISBN: 1-84023-200-5

SPIKE AND DRU
Marsters • Golden •
Sook • Powell
96 page colour paperback
ISBN: 1-84023-282-X

TALES OF THE SLAYERS
Whedon • Sale •
Colan • Russell et al
88 page colour paperback
ISBN: 1-84023-367-2

UNINVITED GUESTS
Watson • Brereton •
Gomez • Florea
96-page colour paperback
ISBN: 1-84023-140-8

STAR WARS

BOBA FETT: ENEMY OF THE EMPIRE
Wagner • Gibson • Nadeau
112-page colour paperback
ISBN: 1-84023-125-4

BOUNTY HUNTERS
Stradley • Truman • Schultz •
Mangels •Nadeau • Rubi •
Saltares
112-page colour paperback
ISBN: 1-84023-238-2

CHEWBACCA
Macan • Various
96-page colour paperback
ISBN: 1-84023-274-9

CRIMSON EMPIRE II
Richardson • Stradley •
Gulacy • Emberlin
160-page colour paperback
ISBN: 1-84023-126-2

DARTH MAUL
Marz • Duursema
96 page colour paperback
ISBN: 1-84023-285-4

EMMISARIES TO MALASTARE
Truman • Lyle
144 page colour paperback
ISBN: 1-84023-336-2

EPISODE I ADVENTURES
152-page colour paperback
ISBN: 1-84023-177-7

INFINITIES: A NEW HOPE
Warner • Johnson •
Snyder • Rio • Nelson
96 page colour paperback
ISBN: 1-84023-432-6

JEDI ACADEMY – LEVIATHAN
Anderson • Carrasco • Heike
96-page colour paperback
ISBN: 1-84023-138-6

JEDI COUNCIL: ACTS OF WAR
Stradley • Fabbr • Della
96 page colour paperback
ISBN: 1-84023-286-2

THE LAST COMMAND
Baron • Biukovic • Shanower
144-page colour paperback
ISBN: 1-84023-007-X

MARA JADE: BY THE EMPEROR'S HAND
Zahn • Stackpole • Ezquerra
144-page colour paperback
ISBN: 1-84023-011-8

OUTLANDER
Truman • Raney
136 page colour paperback
ISBN: 1-84023-287-0

PRELUDE TO REBELLION
Strnad • Winn • Jones
144-page colour paperback
ISBN: 1-84023-139-4

SHADOWS OF THE EMPIRE
Wagner • Plunkett • Russell
160-page colour paperback
ISBN: 1-84023-009-6

TALES: VOLUME 1
Woodring • Marz et al
224 page colour paperback
ISBN: 1-84023-400-8

TALES OF THE JEDI: THE GOLDEN AGE OF THE SITH
Anderson • Gossett •
Carrasco • Heike
144-page colour paperback
ISBN: 1-84023-000-2

TALES OF THE JEDI: REDEMPTION
Anderson • Gossett • Pepoy
112 page colour paperback
ISBN: 1-84023-137-8

TALES OF THE JEDI: THE SITH WAR
152-page colour paperback
ISBN: 1-84023-130-0

TWILIGHT
Ostrander • Duursema •
Magyar
96 page colour paperback
ISBN: 1-84023-399-0

UNDERWORLD: THE YAVIN VASSILIKA
Kennedy • Meglia
120 page colour paperback
ISBN: 1-84023-339-7

UNION
Stackpole • Teranishi •
Chuckry
96-page colour paperback
ISBN: 1-84023-233-1

VADER'S QUEST
Macan • Gibbons • McKie
96-page colour paperback
ISBN: 1-84023-149-1

X-WING ROGUE SQUADRON: THE WARRIOR PRINCESS
Stackpole • Tolson •
Nadeau • Ensign
96-page colour paperback
ISBN: 1-85286-997-6

X-WING ROGUE SQUADRON: IN THE EMPIRE'S SERVICE
Stackpole • Nadeau • Ensign
96-page colour paperback
ISBN: 1-84023-008-8

X-WING ROGUE SQUADRON: BLOOD AND HONOR
Stackpole • Crespo •
Hall • Johnson
96-page colour paperback
ISBN: 1-84023-010-X

X-WING ROGUE SQUADRON: MASQUERADE
Stackpole •Johnson • Martin
96-page colour paperback
ISBN: 1-84023-201-3

X-WING ROGUE SQUADRON: MANDATORY RETIREMENT
Stackpole • Crespo • Nadeau
96-page colour paperback
ISBN: 1-84023-239-0

All publications are available through most good bookshops or direct from our mail-order service at Titan Books. For a free graphic-novels catalogue or to order, telephone 01536 764 646 with your credit-card details or contact Titan Books Mail Order, AASM Ltd., Unit 6, Pipewell Industrial Estate, Desborough, Kettering, Northants., NN14 2SW quoting reference SWVP/GN.

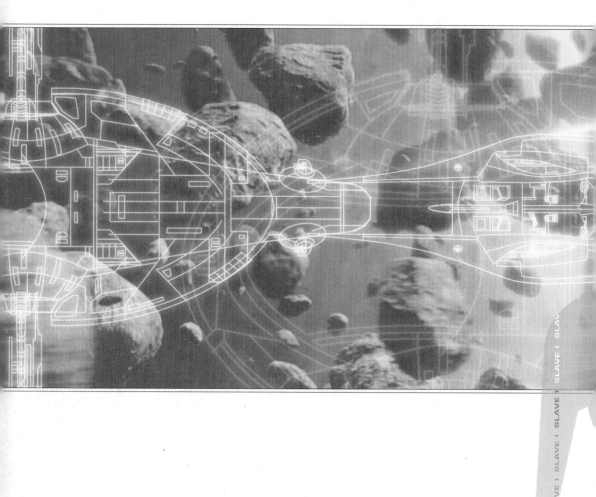